The Beauty of Authenticity

Embracing Your Truth to Live
a Life of Meaning, Purpose, and Grace

Powerful You!
PUBLISHING
Sharing Wisdom ~ Shining Light

THE BEAUTY OF AUTHENTICITY
Embracing Your Truth to Live
a Life of Meaning, Purpose, and Grace

Copyright © 2019

Published by: Powerful You! Inc. USA
powerfulyoupublishing.com

Library of Congress Control Number: 2019937348

Sue Urda and Kathy Fyler – First Edition

ISBN: 978-1-7328128-3-3

First Edition May 2019

Self Help / Women's Studies

Printed in the United States of America

Dedication

This book is for you ~
the individual who is committed
to living their life openly and honestly
as a full expression of their true self.
You are the reason we share these stories, and
we are committed to helping you live authentically.

Table of Contents

Foreword

Follow Your Heart's Authentic Truth

A little over two years ago, I was given the opportunity to be a co-author in one of *Powerful You! Publishing's* anthologies and I said yes to it. I felt deeply called to write books for years but between self-doubt, procrastination, and the loss of all my writings in the San Diego wildfire that took my home in 2007, none of my attempts ever materialized into a published book.

It feels like 10 years has passed in only two, and my memory is a bit fuzzy, but I remember writing for one anthology and then switching to the business book, "Keys to Conscious Business Growth" because I felt guided to. At the time, I was deep into building my coaching business and learning about who I was through some really hard lessons. I fully believed my experience could benefit others in a similar spot.

The funny thing is, at the time, I was an Authenticity Coach who was still really struggling with showing up bigger, flaws and all. Who was I, really? Who would want to read what I had to share? Even though I was excited to finally be writing, I was afraid to be transparent. One of the biggest gifts of the entire process was befriending my soul sister, Sue Urda, one of the most loving and authentic women I know. She and her wonderful partner, Kathy, gently and patiently encouraged and supported me until my story was complete.

Because of their belief in me, I got it done. On February 23, 2016, I became an official best-selling co-author! Looking back, I remember feeling excited about the achievement, yet, regret around what I had written. I also felt the sting of a snarky remark from a "friend" who didn't find value in my story. But the accomplishment was real, it grew me authentically, *and* put me on a path of exponential growth.

Through my own experience, I know for certain when you follow your heart's authentic truth, it's always correct. AND, everything you create along the way, changes as you do. It's like a cool timeline of who you were along the road to who you're becoming, so saying yes to the experience was a huge catalyst in my authentic journey.

And, of course, when Sue reached out and invited me to write the foreword to "The Beauty of Authenticity" (which has been my email address forever), I was elated, excited, and oh, so honored!! My journey the last two years has led me to an unbelievable space of magic and miracles because I've always said yes; yes to following my heart, yes to whatever life brings for my growth, yes to the unknown, and yes to showing up completely transparent in the process. It's the only way you can really get to know and love who you are.

I constantly hear people complain that the word "authenticity" is overused these days, but I believe in order to live life to the fullest, it's something you MUST explore and embrace. True authenticity is being so comfortable in your own skin and with who you are, that nothing can shake you. And that's what this beautiful book is all about.

The stories in this book are treasures that will show you that if you flow with the synchronicities of life, if you allow life to refine you, if you open your arms in surrender to what's meant for you, you will become bolder, bigger, more loving, generous and creative than ever before. You will feel more peace, ease and joy in your life. You will live life on purpose.

You might as well face it. You're unique. You're brilliant. And YOU matter. Without the synchronicities that brought Sue, Kathy, and I together, I wouldn't be here writing this. I wouldn't be the author of a #1 international best-seller, "Your Turning Point," I wouldn't have my own show, *The Mindset Reset Show*, I wouldn't have found my soulmate, Dr. Joe Vitale, and I wouldn't be living the life of my dreams. If you commit to taking the journey of discovering the diamond you truly are, no matter what, then you, too, can experience life beyond your wildest dreams.

The world is waiting for YOU. YOU are the magic. Let your brilliant, beautiful, authentic self shine like the sun.

With love and gratitude,
Lisa Winston
lisaAwinston.com

Introduction

Deciding on the title of this book was a tough call. *The Beauty of Authenticity.* It did not flow easily from us and took weeks to blossom in our minds. Having published eleven anthology books before this one, each of them revolving around the topics of personal empowerment, conscious heart-centered growth, and spiritual awakening for women, we found ourselves perplexed. What topic, what title would resonate with our audience? What subject is yearned for by women everywhere? What single word evokes women and writers to be open to sharing their personal journeys?

And then, it came to us... Authenticity! Yes, this was the theme we were seeking. It seemed silly and incredulous that it took so long for this particular word to reveal itself, because truly we have been on our own authentic journey together—a many years long, sometimes grueling and cruel, drop-to-the-knees, break-open-the-heart journey—of living freely, from our truth, and with meaning, purpose, and grace.

For us, some of this struggle revolved around openly sharing our now twenty-seven-year, happily-coupled, love relationship with significant people in our lives—family, friends, and business associates. While we were mostly received with love, acceptance, and a simple *Okay great*, or *Awwww, good for you two*, or *I was wondering when you were going to mention it*, at times over the years our coupling seemed to drive a wedge in the middle of previously open and thriving relationships. At times it feels sad and heavy; other times freeing and powerful. At all times, it feels authentic and real, and this is the space we choose to live in.

So, when the word *Authenticity* finally popped into our awareness as the perfect title, we both chuckled and said, *Of course. This is it.*

When we started to speak with women about participating as

co-authors in this book, it quickly became apparent that we weren't the only ones who struggled on the way to living authentically. What we heard time and again were stories that had us sighing audibly, laughing out loud, shaking our heads with the knowing of kindred spirits, and getting pangs in our hearts and guts because of the emotional situations, relationships, hurdles, and experiences that were shared with us.

The big question for us was… How could so many women—so many intelligent, successful, benevolent, selfless, caring, high-achieving women—have struggled so long and hard with living as the person they were born to be? Why is it so hard to be authentic? Why is it sometimes hard to be…well…you?

What we found through the stories shared in this book, is that living authentically is not nearly as easy as one would think. C'mon, it should be easy, right? You being you; you showing up as you; you expressing who you are. This should be easier than being someone else, right? Simply do what you think is best to do. Say what you think. Act how you feel. What could be easier than that? Well, now we know you're chuckling with us, because we all know it's not as easy as it sounds or as easy as we'd like it to be—at least not when we first become aware that we haven't been doing it, maybe for our whole lives. And when we become aware and want to make the changes, it sure does help to have a guide or way-shower—you know, someone who's been there and done that.

Truth is, the path to authenticity is not a straight line; it may not be pretty, and in fact, is a continuum and a lifelong journey.

There is judgment in so many forms all around us, and sometimes the cruelest judgment comes from those we love most and those who have our best interest at heart (however misguided it may be). Of course, there's a whole other, much higher level of judgment that comes from within. It shows up as the voice in your head, the well-meaning devil's advocate on your shoulder, or the memories of times past that remind you how embarrassing or painful it can be to show your true colors. You'll find these correlations as you read these stories.

The first common thread among the stories is that no matter what these women endured, or how tough it was to start living freely and from the truth of their spirit, it was always worth it. The deep gratification came swiftly when the co-authors stepped forward, using their inner guidance to light the way, and most often it was richer than they could have imagined.

Another common thread among these co-authors is their newfound clarity of purpose. Each of them will tell you that as they have become more authentic in their lives, they can trust themselves and rely on their own heart whispers above any voice outside themselves.

And finally, these women, without exception, are helping other individuals on their own journeys of authentic living. What does this mean? Well, it's not just one thing; in as much as it's the same, authenticity means something different to everyone. For some, it is finding a new career path even after years of working successfully in a particular field; others up-level, totally revamp, or leave love relationships, friends, or family. And then there are those who, sometimes for the first time in all their years, choose to honor themselves. They begin to put themselves first, cultivate joy in their lives, and rid their space of toxic habits, people, and thoughts. They begin a practice of self-love and acceptance. They begin to rest into their unique and beautiful selves.

Honestly, these women amaze us.

When you read their stories, you'll understand why they chose to share themselves. You'll be moved by their raw personal accounts, their vibrant spirits, and their openness. You'll see yourself in their words, you'll feel how they felt, and you, too, may find yourself choosing to live in the beauty of authenticity.

Namaste`, much love, and deep gratitude,
Sue Urda & Kathy Fyler
Your Publishers

Live Open.
Live Free.

May You Always
Honor the Whispers
Of Your Soul.

Leaving the Critic and Loving the Real Me

Lisa Pezik

Growing up, it seemed I was given a constant stream of directives that encompassed every area of my life.

"Lisa, you will *not* date that boy," I heard, if the object of my affection wasn't white or didn't share my Catholic, American-as-apple-pie background.

"Lisa, you'll go to *this* college and you'll be a nurse. It's a respected profession, and that's what you're doing."

"But I want to be a teacher."

"Oh Lisa, there is no money in teaching. You WON'T do that."

The message was clear: comply or prepare for battle. If I were "smart," I'd do what Mom said, and if I didn't, I got the silent treatment. Off to nursing school I went.

It was an exhausting, extremely rigorous program, so much so that when I came home for my first semester break I slept almost a whole day. When I finally opened my eyes the first thing I saw were the blue-paneled walls that had greeted me each day of my childhood. I could even see some bits of tape here and there, where during my teen years I had affixed pictures of stick-thin models ripped out of magazines. I spent a few minutes absentmindedly peeling the tape off the walls, then headed downstairs to the smell of eggs and bacon cooking.

I was greeted with, "Lisa what's that 'freshman fifteen' thing? Yeah…I think you put on thirty!"

Later that year, it was: "Lisa, are you coming home for summer?"

"No, Mom, I'm working. "

"Lisa, Thanksgiving?"

Nope. I'd work three jobs—as a nursing assistant at the teaching hospital; a college campus tour guide; and resident assistant, just so I didn't have to go home and hear "Lisa…" followed by an insult or an order as to how I was going to live my life.

After graduation, some nursing school friends and I decide to take a vacation to sunny Punta Cana. It's there that I meet Eric.

The first things I notice are the long, lean hunky muscles he had from playing beach volleyball; the meticulous khakis and polo shirt he wore; and the scent of the finest cologne.

But there is much more to him than that. I soon learn he's a well-educated graphic designer, a family man with a good heart, a man who wants children. In just four short days on that beautiful island, we get to know each other on a deeper level than I had ever experienced with anyone.

The catch? He's from Canada, and I'm working as an ICU nurse in a small town in Pennsylvania. Though a long-distance relationship is certainly not ideal, it was better than letting this wonderful person slip away.

Before I know it, we're spending every weekend together. Four whirlwind months later, Eric asks me to marry him.

I pick up the phone to call home and realize that dread, as well as excitement, fills my heart. Not two seconds after I break the news, my mom says, "Oh Lisa, you will both come for Thanksgiving. I insist this time! Your father and I want to meet this man who, well, loves you."

Do I warn Eric? Will that scare him away? Will he understand the challenging relationship I have with my mother?

It's November 26. The football game is playing on the TV and my mom's in the kitchen cutting the turkey with that chainsaw-like electric knife. You can hear that sound from a mile away. That electric knife is probably about as old as me, but it gets the job done. She calls us to the table.

Dad takes his usual place on my right and within minutes is talking about the game and cracking jokes. To my left, Eric is all smiles, but I can't help but think about the future.

My mom is right across the table from me. Maybe, just maybe, a battle won't happen this time.

As I pour and sip, and pour and sip, and pour…and sip…my favourite Cabernet Sauvignon, I realize something. My mom made my favourite stuffing, the spiced candles were lit, table was set, and this is going better than I thought! We're actually having a good time.

I relax a bit and just enjoy dinner. As the turkey is being cleared, Eric says, "Babe, you have to try this pumpkin pie. It's so good."

I accept the pie from his outstretched hand. It is Thanksgiving after all.

Quick as a flash, Mom's head whips around. "Lisa," she shouts, "don't you DARE eat a piece of that pie! Don't you want to fit in your wedding dress? You're going to be too fat to fit into any of them!"

I can't even look to my left. He's going to run. I know it. The first person to love me unconditionally. He's not going to marry into this! I excuse myself from the table and run into my room with the blue-paneled walls.

But there he is, following me up the stairs, wrapping me in his arms.

"What the hell was that?" Eric says. "I'm going to go downstairs to tell her that's NOT OKAY."

Good luck with that, I think. It's better if we just leave.

Later that year, we decide I'm moving. I'm going to break the lease on my apartment, quit my job, and move four hundred miles away to Canada. This long-distance engagement is taking its toll and besides, nothing is keeping me in the US. As an RN, I'm highly employable.

I continue to make weekly calls to my mom. *Be a good girl and call home* runs through my head, week after week, year after year. Then we have our son, Oliver, and everything shifts for me, including my priorities.

I think about the calls home. Maybe they'll change too, I think. We can just talk about Oliver, and she'll let up on me and the extra weight I had been carrying since his birth.

They don't change, though, so I decide to change. Whenever my mom says "Lisa…" on the phone, I just hang up. I don't want to continue with these weekly battles and directives.

The next day I get on the scale to find that something miraculous had happened—I had lost two pounds. Say NO to my mom, three pounds gone. Hang up on her again, another two pounds gone. Over two years and a hundred pounds—GONE!

I start to go to therapy now. I know I can't change the critic, but I can change how I respond. I can change how I feel about myself. Hanging up was the first step, now I stop calling altogether. I throw myself into my family and my work, just like I did while I was in college. I'm going to be okay, I think.

Then one day, just as I'm pulling out of the parking lot after finishing my shift, I hear the ding…ding…ding of text messages, one after the next. That's odd.

My first thought is that something had happened to Eric or Oliver. My heart racing, I pull over and check my phone.

MOM.

Text one: Lisa, we haven't spoken in some time, but I want you to know a few things.

Text two: You are heartless.

Text three: You have no soul.

Text four: No daughter of mine would act like you.

I slam down my phone and put the car back in drive. Though my hands are shaking and hot tears are streaming down my face so I can barely see, something in my gut says, "STOP!"

I hit the breaks, HARD. My seatbelt pounds into my chest, and it feels like slow motion as I look up. A transport truck whooshes by me, just missing my car. Its horn BLARES.

With my hands on my head, the tears streaming, I scream, "Oh my God, Oh my God. No. NO. NO. NO. NO. I could have been killed. I choke back the tears. I…can't…live…like…this…anymore. ENOUGH. Enough is ENOUGH."

Call it Divine Intervention, a jolt of life, a brush with death; that enough-is-enough moment changed everything for me. I couldn't just hang up or call less. I had to do the thing I'd feared the most.

I cut off all contact with my mom. A therapist had told me that I kept drawing the line in the sand, only to step over it. Dig after dig. Fight after fight. Mental health is unpredictable. One day I'm her beautiful daughter, the next day, no longer. I kept apologizing. Kept going back. I couldn't do it anymore.

Through therapy, I realize somewhere in our family lineage it was done to her. She was doing the best she could with what she had.

But I didn't always feel that way. It felt like an excuse. When I first heard that I screamed, "What about me? That doesn't make it okay. That doesn't...make it.... OKAY! So she just gets a pass because she has borderline personality disorder, she's narcissistic and won't get help? That's not FAIR."

I realize that I had to control what I could control and let go of what I couldn't. Then there is the biggest test of all: I have to forgive, or I know the weight will come back on. Gradually, in my own time and in my own way, I learn to forgive my mother, all while recognizing and accepting that it's not healthy for me to have a relationship with her.

After I cut off contact, I put my health, my happiness, and my immediate family first. Our table at home became a safe space, where we talk about anything, we apologize, and we love each other unconditionally. We don't have to be perfect or please.

My professional life also undergoes a major shift at this time. In addition to my job as an RN Educator, I had this side hustle business as an online business strategist and content expert, but I wasn't playing full out. "Lisa, just be happy someone would hire you," rang in my head. The "who do you think you are" demon was strong, but I let go of that belief and start to be more visible. I start a podcast and blog, teach master classes online, and host in-person workshops. I become more active on social media. I create online courses and group coaching programs. I have the confidence to share myself. I find the real me, and I begin to love her. I no longer have to be a "good girl." I no longer have to struggle to gain approval. I don't need the outside world's validation. The only voice I have to listen to is my own.

It is this voice that inspires me to approach my boss with an idea. If I could work from home as an educator and use the online platform I built with my business to teach the nurses, I'd save everyone time, energy, and money, and I could help more people. I am so confident that my boss decides to trust me and let go of the "this is the way it's always been done" mentality so many employers have. She accepts my proposal and I begin to work from home in every aspect of my life, something I've always wanted!

I continue with my self-care routine of healthy eating, regular movement, and therapy. I begin to sleep again.

Ultimately, I shed not only the weight, but also the armor. I turn anger into gratitude and I accept that my upbringing is a gift. It's made me the parent, wife, and strategist I was meant to be.

So I challenge you, don't wait until you've hit your enough-is-enough moment. Fight for your happiness. Fight for your health. Fight for your life. Make a change. Break the mold and re-write the plan.

ABOUT THE AUTHOR: Lisa is an RN, Business Strategist, Thrive Global Author and Worldwide Speaker who studied under thought leaders Brendon Burchard, Bo Eason, and Roger Love. Lisa's unique systems and strategies help her clients take their business online, connect with their target audiences, and convert leads into sales—fast! Her podcast, *The Lisa Pezik Show* exceeds the industry standard, and she's spoken about online business in the US, UK, and Canada. Audiences say Lisa has fiery inspiration, contagious energy, and to-the-point strategies. Her first book, *Break the Mould*, is featured in Chapters Bookstore. Lisa lives in Toronto with her husband Eric, their son Oliver, and three kitties.

Lisa Pezik ~ Global Business Strategist
Speaker, Author, and Content Marketing Expert
lisapezik.com ~ lisa@lisapezik.com
"Grow your business with done for you services from content to cart to cash."

Humiliation:
A Potent Sniffing Salt
Abigail Havermann

It's hard to write about authenticity when you feel like a fraud. Since I was a small child, I've called it as I see it. At seven, I told my mom that my father was an alcoholic. At ten, I spouted off to my grandmother about how her friends were like bagels without cream cheese, boring me into a stupor. I've never had use for small talk and the moment I think I've entered "Pleasantville" in any conversation, I take the first bus out.

I've written volumes about hard lessons learned, told those stories on stages, and taught classes, splaying myself for all to see. My message is how I eventually learned to hear my own voice and live a more authentic life. I've mapped out how all of that has made me a better mother and wife, how I now seem to set boundaries effortlessly instead of throwing up rigid walls or letting people walk all over me like I used to. I had dramatic transformation. I've been told it's inspiring.

So when I decided to participate in this anthology, I thought, no problem. First, I pulled out the story of the number one defining moment in my life, the moment I first realized how loud the toxic voice in my head was. It's a great story: there I was, a practicing couple's therapist, arrested for domestic violence for slapping my drug-addicted husband. I always feel better when I can validate someone else's experience of shame with my own Jerry Springer life.

My arrest occurred the day before I was planning to take my two-year-old and leave my husband for good, but rather than spending the day packing, I was cuffed in the mid-morning light with neighbors peering through their curtains, no doubt questioning any relationship advice I had ever given them.

There was the strip search, the moment I learned I'd be staying the night, and the crowning mortification: the attorney my dad sent to the jail to see me was exactly my age and from my home town (which, by the way, was *across the country*). Oh, all the people we knew in common!

The climax of this story has me lying on a hard slab of plastic in the middle of an overcrowded jail cell with four bunk beds filled by eight other women. It was there that I allowed my intuitive voice out of the soundproof box where it had lived nearly since it was born. Mostly, I ruminated on why I ever married John (his name has been changed to protect his privacy) in the first place. He wasn't ambitious, he wasn't social, he was too old for me and I wasn't sure I had ever been attracted to him. Then, out of nowhere this toxic voice came hurling up to my frontal lobe from the back of my skull and said, "Well, who else was going to love you?"

For the first time I understood that I had been following this voice around like the Pied Piper for nearly thirty years. Decent story, right? I tried to end the essay with, "That liar put me in jail, and I knew I'd never listen to my toxic voice again." That's how I always tell the story on stage. But this time, the ending fell flat. I gave it to an editor friend who suggested I revisit the first lines to get closer to my thesis: how I stopped listening to my toxic voice. *Nothing.* I meditated. I wrote it twelve different ways. I stepped away from it. I came back to it.

I decided this must be the wrong story. I needed to write a different one. This time I picked when I came to Jesus (not really, I'm Jewish, but you get the point) and in a conflagration of humiliation, admitted to myself I cared more about what other people thought of me than being honest with myself. Now *that* was an awesome story. My husband caught on fire at my professional holiday party by leaning against a candle in a window. He was on so much Oxycotin that he didn't feel it. Everyone else was also unaware until another guest saw him go aflame from the outside walkway, burst inside, and tackled John to the ground.

What I find juiciest about that story is the envy that was seeping from my pores when we arrived at the hosts' large Denver Tudor home. The entire first floor was covered with a white carpet one could only compare to a cloud. It was more expensive than my and John's cars combined and more comfortable than our bed. I desperately wanted to impress this woman so she would send me referrals, and by the end of the night her carpet had a four-by-four dusty gray stain—the proverbial elephant in the room, miming my disaster of a marriage. The stain would have confined to a few black streaks, had I not gotten on all fours in my skirt and heels and stockings and tried to rub it out with a wet rag, while the other guests continued sipping their drinks and tasting slabs of salami from the antipasto on the table just above me. My efforts had only made the carpet worse, not unlike how I had made myself infinitely more miserable in my marriage by trying to cover for and control my husband's behavior and addiction.

I had gotten to the bottom of that story with just enough words left for a neat explanation of how my life transformed after that night and how I now live my life with full and constant integrity, being true to myself, blah blah blah. Only, first of all, my life didn't transform after that night. In fact, it was six weeks *after* that night that I found myself on the floor of that jail cell begging the Universe for mercy, seriously questioning if Jesus may in fact be able to help me (just kidding, Nana).

Now the deadline for this essay is approaching and I couldn't understand why these stories weren't serving the purpose they always have, exemplifying how I stepped into myself, teaching the importance of identifying and adjusting the volume on our intuitive and toxic voices. These stories had led to a rebirth—my divorce, remarriage, a new career as a financial consultant, finding myself. Yet, every time I tried to tie them up into a tight moral, they unraveled like yarn stuck to a cat's claw.

Then today it hit me. It all came back to Lydia, a new prospect I had met with two weeks ago. I immediately loved Lydia—smart, funny, independent, a fabulous foreign accent. Even better, I knew I had what she needed; I knew I could be of value to her. I laid out a financial plan that could protect her money and ensure she'd have enough for the rest of her life. It was very exciting (if you get excited about that sort of thing). I feared she was vulnerable to making less-than-ideal investment choices, for the wrong reasons, not to mention falling prey to someone who didn't have her best interests at heart. There are so many shady people in my business.

But. I also got excited about taking her on as a new client. I got excited about the sale. I went too fast in the meeting, hoping to "close," and I confused and overwhelmed her with information. Not only did I not close, she might cancel her next appointment possibly leaving her retirement at risk. This sent me spiraling.

For the last two weeks I've been marinating in shame, or rather shame is marinating my insides. My gut is bathing in it like the flank steak soaking in Teriyaki sauce in my fridge. On the days I wake up and my gut feels empty and pure I whisper a silent prayer of gratitude to the Universe, but I tread lightly because I know the toxic feeling could be just around the corner. An attack like this never confines itself to one space, either. It leaks. When the phone rings at work I say out loud, "Oh shit," because my first assumption is someone is mad at me, I've screwed something up, a client wants to fire me.

I thought I had beat it. My life has been altered by the very stories I planned to share in this essay. I upgraded husbands by two-thousand-fold. I worked on my nagging and critical nature to the extent that my sixteen-year-old now confides in me almost daily and actually seems to value my input. I am walking through the devastation of my eight-year-old's recently diagnosed neuromuscular disorder with an amount of grace, faith, and levelheadedness I didn't know I had in me. I am running a successful business, the second business I have built, and have the luxury of only working with people I love. All of this is because of the miles I've run (and in some cases, limped), and the lessons I learned. Because I dared to be awakened, show up in my life, and change course.

So why is this essay so hard to write? Here's why: the story of going to jail is about turning down the volume on my toxic voice, an epiphany that fundamentally changed my life. Unfortunately, I've been listening to that very voice nonstop since I met with Lydia.

The fire story is about being exposed, trying to look great when all Hell was breaking loose. But I've been slinking around singing my old childhood tune, "Nobody likes me, everybody hates me, might as well eat worms," for two weeks, so it's no wonder I couldn't write a neat, pretty ending about how now all is well. Once again I deceived myself (and was trying to deceive you), while secretly soaking in self-loathing.

So I come full circle. Authenticity to me is about my willingness to be awake to my success and my struggle. It's about daring to show up in the world as I am, on days when I feel inspired and proud, and on days like today when I have to cop to the shitstorm brewing inside me. Forty-eight seems too old to be weathering days like this. I thought I'd be done punishing myself by now. Dare I tell you that I am still capable of comparing my insides to others' outsides and despairing my way into a bottle of wine and way too much chocolate?

Shame is a reaction I have to showing up in the world. I can have it as easily when I am successful as I can when I'm a failure. When the first occurs I think to myself "Who do you think you are?" When I fail, I tell myself "What did you expect?" And when I crawl under a rock, I experience a different kind of shame—I am not living my life's purpose, I am not doing what I was put here to do, so dedicating myself to binge-watching Netflix and never risking being seen isn't an option either.

So this is my truth. I made a mistake. My desire to close a deal got in the way of my greater good, it got in the way of my mission. I hate admitting that. I hate being human. I'd like to say I'm one-hundred percent altruistic, all the time. I'd like to say I never fall prey to the twinge of competition, or the hollering of my ego. I'd like to tell you I never lose it on my kids or bribe my husband with sexual favors. But to say all that would be inauthentic. Instead I will say that The Universe has a way of stuffing sniffing salt up my nose to see how quickly I'll open my eyes. These days I come to more readily, and with a healthier dose of self-compassion. I'm not going to lie; there are times it feels like a curse. But then I remember that I'll take awake over painless eight days a week. Maybe someday I'll master both.

ABOUT THE AUTHOR: Abby Havermann is a psychotherapist turned Financial Consultant. Through writing, speaking, and consulting, she empowers women to root out, hear, and ultimately *listen* to their authentic voice. Having spent years milling around in both her own psyche and those of her therapy clients, Abby brings perspective and purpose to the financial planning process. Using her own mistakes as a guide, along with a good dose of humor, she seeks to align women with their personal and financial freedom. She and her husband own their own boutique financial planning firm and have clients across the United States.

Abigail Havermann
Havermann Financial Services, Inc.
havermannfinancial.com
abby@havermannfinancial.com
303-463-0436

The Pivot

Who Told Us Our Best Life Was in a Straight Line?

Shannon Sedlacek

I don't normally remember my dreams, so one night back in September of 1994 when I dreamed I fell off my ladder while painting my house, I took notice. Just before waking, I got a glimpse of myself lying in a hospital bed, seriously hurt. It wasn't just my physical injuries that caught my attention, but the timing. That day I planned to paint my house using the very ladder I fell from in my dream.

I woke up sweaty, disoriented, and unclear where I was. Not certain if what I dreamed was real or not, I patted my body, checking it for injuries. Satisfied that I was unhurt, I concluded it was just a dream and started my day.

Although the dream was unsettling, it never occurred to me to cancel the painting project, or even postpone it. Back then, my life was organized and structured around keeping busy. As a litigation attorney working sixty to eighty hours a week this was an easy goal to meet. Time off was not part of my routine. Not that I didn't love vacations; I was just too busy to take them. Even weekends meant nothing, and although other associates and I hid from partners on Friday afternoons to avoid getting last-minute assignments we often came in on Saturdays and Sundays anyway. We even bragged about our lack of sleep and the stupendous hours we were billing. We all had our sights set on making partner, but for me it went much deeper than that.

Painting my house didn't count as time off because it would keep me busy and distracted. Being busy enabled me to ignore the whispers in my head. Those whispers wanted me to have painful conversations that a part of me knew I needed to have and the other part feared would destroy everything I had worked for. I carefully guarded my success, and whenever those whispers crept in, I turned to my three best friends: Avoidance, Denial, and Distraction.

The success model I religiously adhered to was the Gerbil Wheel. It's simple. You get on the Gerbil Wheel and start running. You run faster. The object is to keep the wheel moving.

Like all methods, the Gerbil Wheel had its pros and cons. I loved it because it led to the accomplishments I needed to gain others' love and approval. It also kept me so exhausted that even when I wasn't spinning, I was still avoiding my life like a champion. It never occurred to me that the constant action required was not sustainable.

What was I working so hard to avoid? Misalignment between my inner and outer lives. The very act of acknowledging this divergence would require me to admit my life was a complete lie. That's tough to do. In my outer life, everything looked great. I was a highly paid attorney in a prestigious law firm and worked for a great boss; I also owned my home, had wonderful friends, pets that loved me, and I was living with a fabulous guy who wanted to marry me. I had checked off all the boxes on my imaginary success checklist.

Only it wasn't working. I was exhausted trying to maintain my façade of success, and I was miserable.

The Gerbil Wheel was finally taking its toll. I no longer wanted to work sixty to eighty hours a week, and faking enthusiasm for it was becoming increasingly challenging. There were days I did not want to get out of bed. I wanted to have weekends to play. I also wanted to kiss my secretary, which presented a whole other set of problems for me.

I was afraid if anyone knew I was gay they wouldn't love me anymore. My friends wouldn't want to hang out with me. My family would reject me, and my boyfriend would leave me. I might even get fired. This fear of full-scale rejection kept me on the Gerbil Wheel, running toward the illusion of a perfect life and away from my authentic self.

My devotion to achievement came from my belief I needed to earn both love and approval. This started back in grade school. I grew up Catholic, went to Catholic grade school, and attended mass with my family every Sunday. The church taught me being gay meant I was fundamentally flawed, so I began using achievement to fill the hole created by the feeling that I wasn't good enough or lovable. If I could win the approval of adults and friends, I could cover up my "fundamental flaw." When earning blue ribbons, trophies, and medals were not enough, I moved to degrees, certifications, and awards. I became an attorney to earn the approval and love of my parents, teachers, and friends. It was like a stock plan. If I invested enough in "achievement banking" I would have so much stock in approval they might still love me once my flaws were discovered.

Keeping busy was key to maintaining my "portfolio"; that's why it never occurred to me to cancel or postpone the painting project. But the wariness I had over the dream didn't go away with my first cup of coffee. As the morning progressed, I replayed the dream enough times to realize why it was still bothering me. The reason I fell off the ladder wasn't that I was being chased or pushed by a bad guy. I fell off the ladder *because of me*. In my dream, I made choices that caused me to fall. The fact that those choices were consistent with what I would do in real life made the dream all the more frightening.

Several days prior to my dream, I was puzzling over how to paint my staircase. The only way to reach the highest side wall was to turn the ladder tip, placing it against the side wall. But this created another problem: only one foot of the ladder would rest on the stair while the other foot would dangle in midair. In my dream, I reassured myself I could paint by keeping my weight shifted so the one ladder foot was firmly planted on the stairs. In my dream, I climbed the ladder with one foot completely unsupported. The choice to push forward, rather than slowing down to seek other solutions summed up my life story. It was the constant action of the Gerbil Wheel being played out in my dream! My decision to place the ladder in a position that was at best precarious led to a serious injury. Though I knew this, I decided blaming my fall on the awkwardness of the steep staircase or the defectiveness of the ladder was far easier than taking any personal responsibility. I was, after all, an attorney, and a professional fault-finder.

I was concerned enough, however, to change my strategy. I decided I would avoid the stairs; I even promised my boyfriend before he left for work that I would not paint them. And I kept that promise. I started out conservatively, painting with my feet firmly planted on the ground—no heights and no ladders involved. After gaining some confidence, I graduated to using a small two-step ladder. I figured if I fell, I couldn't get hurt. After getting comfortable on the short step ladder, I began using the six-foot-high ladder.

By mid-morning, the intensity of the dream had receded. It was a gorgeous sunny day, so I decided to take advantage of the weather and finish up some exterior painting. I retrieved the extension ladder —the same extension ladder I fell off in my dream—and extended it to its full twelve-foot reach. I leaned it against the second story back deck. I climbed to the top of the ladder and began to paint the lattice work above the deck.

I don't remember falling.

I don't remember grabbing for something, trying to stop the fall.

I don't remember being in the air.

I do remember the impact.

When my back slammed into the ground from about sixteen feet above, I remember feeling surprised that my attempts to avoid the consequences of my dream had failed. I had managed to seriously injure myself. Then everything went black.

Warm dog kisses woke me up. Groggy and unsure of what happened, I was still embracing denial. I didn't want to be injured. Recovery from an injury meant stillness, the stillness I'd been avoiding for years while I ran on my Gerbil Wheel. I knew stillness would bring reflection and pain, so I refused to call 911 and prevented neighbors and friends from doing so as well. In my mind, I wasn't seriously injured if I didn't need emergency help. Eventually, my injuries landed me in the same hospital bed I'd dreamed of earlier that morning.

After I was discharged, barely able to shuffle-step from my bed to my couch, I began my long, painful recovery. Mostly, I had to lay down, stay still, and listen as the conversations I'd been avoiding came roaring to life.

How do you tell a guy who wants to marry you that you might be gay? My utterly awkward beginning, "Hey, can I talk with you for a sec?" certainly belied the enormity of this life-changing conversation. I told him I had been doing a lot of thinking since I fell off the ladder, then I revealed the deep, dark secret I was sure would lead to my demise. He listened, then offered me a response that was both clear and unequivocal: he loved me and he would give me the space I needed to figure this out. If I was straight, he still wanted to marry me; if I was gay, he wanted to be my friend.

After years of self-rejection, hearing those words was like being bathed in sunlight and honey. They were bright and sweet and amazing. His love was without conditions. There was no need to earn it. He wasn't demanding that I do or be anything in order to gain his approval. Though I had hurt him, albeit unintentionally, he gave me the gift that changed the course of my life—the gift of unconditional love.

This love allowed me to see I am not fundamentally flawed. Yes, I have flaws like anybody, but they do not make me unlovable. When he told me he loved me no matter what, I allowed myself, perhaps for the first time, to love me as well.

That fall from the ladder ultimately taught me I would never be able to fill up a hole with approval and achievement, though my efforts were epic. That hole wasn't fillable because it had never existed in the first place.

The part of me that still might seek approval would love to tell you I never got on the Gerbil Wheel again. But that isn't true. The Wheel still calls to me, and occasionally I climb on board. The difference is I now know to ask myself what I am avoiding that I think being busy will fix.

Other amazing, unimaginable things happened after I embraced my authentic self. My Catholic parents walked me down the aisle at my wedding to my wife, many years before it was legal. They invited their Catholic family friends, who also came and supported us at our wedding. I felt the love and support of my best friends, who stood next to me on the bow of the ship as we exchanged vows. Although my brother and his family refused to attend, the massive rejection I feared never materialized. Sure, the rejections hurt, but not nearly as bad as the pain I inflicted on myself while trying to avoid who I was.

I also recovered from my physical injuries, left the practice of law, and became a professional firefighter. This, after I used to joke that I spent my busiest days as an attorney "putting out fires."

Now retired from firefighting, my life is dedicated to igniting or rekindling fires in others as a transformational coach so that they can courageously step into living the best version of themselves. Take it from me, dreams do come true—literally. We must only be still enough to listen.

ABOUT THE AUTHOR: Shannon Sedlacek, a speaker, writer, former litigation attorney and firefighter, and transformational coach, is no stranger to challenges. After initially failing out of the academy, she went on to become an award-winning firefighter at age thirty-nine. She overcame harassment, discrimination, and bullying in the workplace to become the first female officer ever in her department; endured failed IVF to become the mother of an adopted son; and became a licensed private pilot after vomiting during the flight test. Using humor, creativity, and bold action, Shannon helps her clients redefine their own challenges as necessary building blocks for success. Her motto: Be. You. Optimally.

Shannon Sedlacek, Speaker & Coach
Be. You. Optimally.
shannonsaid.com
shannon@insightfulfirefighter.com
206-486-6201

The Life Surfer
DeAnne Gauya

It was May 13, 2010. I was at a meeting with my father, the President and sole-owner of Hylie Products, Inc., our family's manufacturing business; the Vice President, who had worked at Hylie since coming to America from Portugal some thirty-five years earlier; and Nitesh, our Contract Manager from Proctor & Gamble (P&G). The four of us were sitting at a long table in a conference room at Duracell International Headquarters in Bethel, Connecticut, about to renegotiate a contract for one hundred percent of the 9-volt battery terminal production for the entire North American market. My grandfather, a Master Toolmaker and Engineer who had started Hylie in 1958, designed this terminal. He had passed away ten years earlier at the age of ninety-one, and that's when my father took over.

This one contract with Duracell, which was owned by P&G, had been held by Hylie for over thirty years and represented $2 million of our 2.3 million annual revenue. Now, I am not great at math, but I guessed that this contract was equal to about ninety percent of Hylie's work.

I did not work at Hylie; in fact, I didn't have much to do with the business at all. I was at this critical meeting as my father's only child and successor in owning the business, an event which was to take place far into the future, perhaps ten to twenty years. Or so I thought.

"If you want to keep a three-year contract for one hundred percent of the North American market for Duracell batteries," Nitesh told us, "you need to become a Women's Business Enterprise (WBE) and become part of the P&G Supplier Diversity Program." Nitesh glanced at me, then looked at my father and the VP. "You two need to make her the CEO, majority owner, and make her happy. If you don't do this, P&G will not renew your contract."

I sat there for a moment, stunned and completely blindsided. My breath got short and labored; my heart was pounding like a roll on a kettle drum. What was happening? My inner voice was screaming, NO! This path is terrible for you, DeAnne! Do not go down it!

Of course, I couldn't say any of this out loud, so I told them I would have to think about the proposal and get back to Nitesh with my decision. All the while, my gut was screaming, flipping, getting all knotted up. NOOOOOOO...

You see, I had no experience working in manufacturing, and no desire to. I had no desire to work for any company. The mere idea— sitting at a desk all day, wearing tight, stuffy business attire, going to meetings filled with posturing, bullshit, red tape, bureaucracy, and surrounded by men from whom I had to win respect and recognition —sounded more like a prison sentence than a job.

It also meant giving up my own work as an entrepreneur, which I still loved after twenty-two years. I was a free spirit, a "One Woman Show," the sole proprietor of my holistic fitness and stress reduction business. My days consisted of personal training—both for individuals and groups, teaching yoga, providing massage therapy, and speaking and writing about my passion—holistic fitness. I loved helping people improve their health and wellbeing. I loved the variety of activities, the ability to call all the shots, and determine my work mix.

Since late November 2009, I had been living my dream life as a single mother and breadwinner for myself and my two children, eight-year-old Justin and six-year-old Katharine. We had a beautiful home in a lakefront community that was described by many as, "a paradise for children," because of the numerous, year-round activities for them. I had just purchased a property for my holistic fitness and stress reduction business less than a minute from my children's school. My plan was to establish my own retreat center: The Dancing Star Center for Stress Reduction.

My mantra was "Heal yourself, heal the world," and my vision was to offer holistic services that nurtured healing from the inside out and opened hearts and minds to inspire people to move toward more peaceful and loving ways of being in the world. It was my dream. I felt divinely inspired. I enjoyed the peace and quiet of working in a small cottage in the middle of the woods in a rural town. I was eventually going to build a yurt in the woods with a big wooden platform so that my students could practice yoga and be one with nature. I saw my Center as the way to successfully balance my work with being a good single parent.

I was highly trained. I had decades of experience. I had successfully transplanted my business three times and was still extremely passionate about my mission. I was, to quote Rumi, "Letting the beauty we love be what we do. There are hundreds of ways to kneel and kiss the ground." I had found mine at the age of sixteen. I did not need help "figuring out the color of my parachute." I KNEW.

Back to Hylie Products, Inc. and my Duracell decision. Should I become the CEO and majority owner of my family manufacturing business and give up my lifelong career and passion or not? I had to decide quickly. P&G had to know. Our contract was expiring in six weeks.

When I turned to my close friends and then-boyfriend, I heard, "Who wouldn't want to be a CEO? Are you crazy?"; "How could you even think of letting your family and all of the Hylie employees down?"; "You can't be selfish, DeAnne."; "This is for your children and your beloved grandfather."; "This will give you security and pay your bills."; "Screw what you are passionate about doing."; and finally, "You have to do this."

I heard what everyone was saying and it made sense, but my intuition was still saying NO! Maybe it wasn't screaming as loudly as it initially had, before being stifled by the opinions and logic of others, but it was clear. There was no ambivalence when it came to my gut.

Before I knew it decision time had arrived. Did I trust my gut or listen to everyone and do "The Right Thing?"

The Right Thing won out. I told them I would accept the CEO position and become the majority owner of Hylie; I would give up the career I had worked for over two decades to build. I sold my retreat center, sold my house, and lost several hundred thousand dollars in real estate. (I sold when the housing market and mortgage industry collapsed.) I also switched my children's schools, and we moved forty-five minutes away to a condominium, all so I could run Hylie Products.

What was working at Hylie Products like for me? It was HELL. My father who was supposed to step down, retire, and let me take over, did not keep up his end of the bargain. "DeAnne", he told me when I started, "it's like being pushed off of a dock. You will have to learn to swim."

Little did I know that he would become a ball and chain, continually trying to drown me. He not only stayed at the company, but at the same office and the same desk, which was at a ninety-degree angle three feet from me, where he sat listening to and second-guessing me from day one. The rest of the environment was not much better. It was noisy, chaotic, male-dominated, and filled with dysfunction, blurred boundaries, negativity, and toxicity. The company was stuck back in the 1970s—maybe 1980s,—but was certainly not in the twenty-first century!

Turning the company around and keeping them afloat was going to take a Herculean effort. There were many obstacles to overcome but I remained determined. After all, I had faced many challenges before. I was smart. I worked hard. I could do this. I did my best to embrace my new career, but my intuition still whispered, "This isn't for you, DeAnne." Every day I felt like a fake, an imposter. Being the CEO of a business that I had no passion for or experience with was just not me.

Fast forward seven years. It's now 2017 and I am a stressed-out, anxious, miserable mess. Most nights, I am drinking too much to numb myself. I have recurrent dreams that I'm driving a car straight up a ninety-degree cliff. I almost get to the top and then the car starts to flip over backward and I wake up panting and in a cold sweat. My colleagues tell me that I need to try an anti-anxiety drug.

My children don't like their totally stressed-out Mommy. I am leaving them, once again, on my way to JFK Airport for a flight to California for a Biomedical Device Manufacturing Show when I tell the driver to stop the car. I just can't get on the plane. I am having a full-out panic attack. My heart is racing. My breath is short and labored. My head is spinning and I feel like I am going to die.

I get back to my condo and decide that I have to get out of this. Nothing is worth my mental, physical, and emotional health. I have to listen to my gut and go back to being a solo Fitness Entrepreneur and Stress Reduction Expert. I attend the IDEA, Personal Trainer Institute East in College Park, Maryland, and the workshop, "The Online Fitness Frontier" with marketing expert and fitness business coach, Vito La Fata.

In early June 2017, I resigned from Hylie. I gave up my title, my interest in the company and sold my stocks back to my father, the VP and the employees. I gave back the business I had never wanted in the first place.

Today, I am, once again, doing what I always have loved. I feel like The Phoenix rising from the ashes, like the lotus ready to bloom. I am living what Brendon Burchard, one of the most-watched personal development trainers in the world, refers to as the "Charged Life". I feel genuine and realize that for the first time in years, I feel happy, comfortable in my own skin, and all without the aid of anti-anxiety medication. I have become what I call a successful "Life Surfer."

As I write this, I am reminded of a Derek Walcott poem that I heard Jon Kabat Zinn read at a conference I attended in Arlington, Virginia back in 1993. I will leave you with his words.

Love After Love

The time will come
when, with elation, you will greet yourself arriving
at your own door, in your own mirror
and each will smile at the other's welcome,

and say, sit here. Eat.
You will love again the stranger who was our self.
Give wine. Give bread. Give back your heart
to itself, to the stranger who has loved you

all your life, whom you ignored for another, who knows you by
heart.
Take down the love letters from the bookshelf,

the photographs, the desperate notes,
peel your own image from the mirror.
Sit. Feast on your life.

ABOUT THE AUTHOR: DeAnne C. Gauya, MS, CPT, LMT, NCBTMB, E-RYT 200 is a writer, speaker and the Creative Energetic Orchestrator (CEO) of Gauyafit, LLC, "a one-woman show" dedicated to empowering Mid-lifers and Active Agers to decrease stress, increase joy, and become confident "Life Surfers." She currently works with individuals and groups of all ages and fitness levels, both offline and online, and has had clients in The White House, the Entertainment Industry, and the Arts. DeAnne is a single mom to two teenage children, two cats, and a turtle. She enjoys learning new things, spending time at the beach and traveling. Currently in her mid-50s, she plans on living life to the fullest until 90 or so.

DeAnne C. Gauya
GAUYAFIT, LLC
gauyafit.com
DeAnne@gauyafit.com
203-525-2545

No More Hiding

Learning to Embrace Perfect Imperfections
Erica Martinez

W hen I was five years old, I went off to kindergarten like most kids. I also received my very first report card. Most people probably couldn't recall this particular event; they certainly wouldn't view it as significant. I, on the other hand, remember it in vivid detail. Why? Because like many little eager people-pleasers, I wanted to be a good girl and get good grades and make my parents proud.

I remember bringing home that rectangular manila envelope and handing it to my mother. I remember her looking it over, smiling bigger and bigger, until, as she neared the bottom of the page, her face tensed up ever so slightly.

Mama? Mama, what's wrong?

Nothing, sweetheart.

But mama, you're frowning.

It's nothing.

Mama! Just tell me.

Well...

What, Mama?

Well, you're doing excellent in all of your subjects.

Okay?

But...

But, what Mama?

It's just...

Just tell me, Mama. Please!

Well, your teacher has just one little note about an area to improve.
Okay, Mama. What is it?
She says…(wrinkling up her face)
You are TOO TALKATIVE!

Everything stopped. I remember a stillness and yet a crazy beating of my heart, like it would come out of my chest. I was utterly defeated, flattened, the wind knocked completely out of my five-year-old sails. How could this happen? I am not a good girl. I am not making my mama proud. I am not making anyone proud. I am *too much*.

From then on, I went from too talkative to almost silent. I stopped ordering for myself at restaurants, which made my father crazy. Picture frustrated man screaming at sobbing little girl. I have no idea what he was thinking, but now that I am a parent I'm guessing he just didn't know what else to do. How would any parent know how to navigate this abrupt change in their previously exuberant and outgoing little girl's behavior? Poor Dad!

Although I certainly didn't know it then, I believe this was THE moment I discovered that other people will label and define us whether we want them to or not. I don't believe my teacher was mean-spirited. She likely believed little girls needed to be quieter to navigate life and be accepted. Perhaps that was her own story of growing up. Perhaps she thought she was helping me. In any event, I doubt she had any clue as to the consequences her words might have.

Nonetheless, that moment started me down a particular path that I can only now see in retrospect. Instead of allowing myself to be chatty and talkative and full of crazy little girl energy, I started to self-modulate. I started to dampen my frequency. I started to dim that flame in my little heart. I started to believe that I needed to be less in order to fit in.

Strangely, though I was barely speaking, I continued to believe that I was still too much and too talkative and too everything. On top of that—I began stuffing food into my mouth. I don't know if the food made me feel better or if I was just trying to shove things in my mouth to keep the real me from coming out. Regardless, every time I found myself in a new situation with unclear expectations I compensated by overeating and hiding out. Seemingly overnight, I went from an active, thin little girl to a chubby, shy one. I continued to dream of being in the spotlight, yet I chose to hide rather than face the recrimination of my peers or teachers.

In third grade I started a new school and found myself the proverbial fish out of water. I knew no one, and there were cliques and dynamics that I just did not fit into or understand. On top of that, it was a school for "gifted" kids; upon the recommendation of my last teacher I had taken the test for the program and made the cut. Now, instead of being the smartest one in the room, I was simply the new kid.

I remember one particularly awful day where we were each made to stand up and recite our multiplication tables. When it was my turn, I failed—badly. For one, I was painfully shy and hated to speak in school. For another, I had no clue how to do multiplication. We had not started that at my old school. I sat back down, red-faced and horribly embarrassed as other kids snickered and called me dumb. I remember coming home and sobbing uncontrollably. I was used to being "too much"; I was not used to being labeled dumb. Lucky for me, my grandfather was my afternoon caregiver. When I told him what happened he gave me a hug, a twinkie, and a math lesson. We practiced every day after school until I had it down. I learned my math, I had love and support, and I had my sugary treat.

While this was a victory of sorts, the story did not have a happy ending. As I grew in confidence and started to show up again, I was taken down a peg by my peers. I mean, no one likes a "little miss know it all," do they? I had become so good at math that I was one of the smartest again and could answer the questions. Unfortunately, my longing to fit in was stronger than my power to be myself and own my abilities. I stopped raising my hand and hid what I knew. I learned I needed to make room for others to shine by sacrificing my own light. I got so good at this that teachers were often surprised when they called on me and I had the right answer.

Just recently I realized that I had deeply imprinted this negative belief about "know it alls" while guest teaching at my daughter's third grade class. I found myself frustrated by a little girl who could not help but wildly throw her hand up to answer all the questions. I judged her so harshly in my own head, thinking she should self-edit, that she should be less. It was awful, and even as I write about it now, it is difficult to swallow the hypocrisy. I want to say to that girl, *You go, you beautiful soul, you raise your hand high! Don't you dare stop being you just because I was mortified to be me.*

I continued to hide well into adulthood. On my first day as a teacher, I was so terrified that I would do something wrong I sat amongst the students and allowed someone else to take over the class. I needed someone to emulate before I could even think about getting up there. Turns out, she wasn't any better than me. She didn't know things that I didn't know. She didn't even seem that confident. After that, I started to realize that I was good enough; I didn't need other people's words. I was allowed to be my own person and teach the way I wanted to teach. This—the idea that people would have to accept me, flaws and all—was a shocking revelation to me. I didn't have to be someone else. I could just be me. How novel!

Still, that darn programming of not being enough/too much was pretty hardwired, and I continued to lose myself every single time there was a period of transition or a new role. I would begin each new journey by behaving how I imagined I should rather than just being me. I continued to self-modulate. I continued to have someone else's frequency and energy level. Many times, I would even hear someone else's words coming out of my mouth.

Not surprisingly, when in 2011 I received my very first 360 evaluation, there were numerous inconsistencies. In a 360, you self-assess, people who report to you get to assess you, and then your supervisor assesses you. Any areas of mismatch became a topic of the subsequent conversation, and I was horribly misperceived across several areas.

Why? Because I was acting like I thought I should rather than who I actually am. Of course, it caused a mismatch! Light bulb moment. *Do not do as you imagine others to do—just do you!* I already knew this. And yet, there I was. New role, new opportunity to feel like a complete imposter. So, I hid myself and I continued to overeat.

This horrific cycle went on FOREVER! Seriously, every time I would encounter the unknown, my pattern of overeating and hiding the real me kicked into high gear. It was like I just couldn't stop myself. I think the food was shoving down all the insecurities I had around showing up as my true self. It was like in the third grade—I was scared and afraid and super self-conscious that if I was myself, rather than who I thought I was supposed to be, I would never be accepted. And I was still desperate to be accepted.

So how did I uncover my truth? For some people, a milestone birthday does the trick, setting off all kinds of shifts and changes; for others, a major loss serves as catalyst. I had both. It was 2016, I was turning 40 (and not living my life as I'd imagined) when my dad, just sixty-one, died suddenly from a heart attack.

My father and I had a special bond. He was not just my parent, he was my best friend. When we talked, which was pretty much every day, it was like talking to myself. There was nothing we couldn't talk about and though he was loving and supportive, he did not hold back on the criticism when he thought I needed it. His death shook my world to its core.

But as awful as that was, it was a blessing too. I stopped caring about being "too much" and I really stopped caring about what other people thought. I started learning a whole lot more about me and what I wanted out of life, which included taking control of what went into my mouth and how I showed up in the world. I started taking a more active role, rather than passively accepting what was given. I took my journey into my own hands.

This meant leaving my job, which had become a source of burn-out, and starting my own business. Instead of living according to other people's labels or expectations, I would now create my own labels and follow my own path. Now, I work towards being the role model my little girl and so many other little girls (and women) in this world need. Today, I am a coach and a teacher and I help others learn to burn brighter.

This is only a slice of my story, but hopefully it is enough to help others understand why I am so passionate about what I do. I want everyone to know that what they think and feel is important. I want them to set aside other people's labels and expectations and feel empowered to pick their own path and live a life bigger than they think possible.

I want *you* to know and feel in every cell in your body that YOUR VOICE MATTERS.

ABOUT THE AUTHOR: Dr. Erica Martinez is a Registered Nurse, entrepreneur, coach, storyteller, and wellness enthusiast. She is the Founder and President of NutriSherpa, where she helps clients find their voice and take back control over their lives. Erica recognizes that we all find ourselves in various roles throughout life (wife, mother, boss, nurse, educator, fill in your own blank) where we can easily become overwhelmed; however, we can also learn to thrive. She has a unique approach that empowers clients to burn brighter rather than burn out. Erica is a Midwestern girl at heart but currently lives in Southern California with her husband, two kids, and dog.

Dr. Erica Martinez, RN
NutriSherpa, LLC
nutrisherpa.com
facebook.com/nutrisherpa
714-900-2002

The Knitting
Liz Powell

"Look, Mum! I figured it out!"

I held up the half-knitted sleeve so my bedridden mother could see my handiwork. She had begun work on this cardigan some months previous, having admired one I'd made several years earlier in the same pattern. She'd chosen a delicate, dusty pale green shade, and I found myself secretly wishing she were making it for me rather than for herself. She'd lovingly worked the front, back, and one sleeve. But as the cancer had slowly taken hold of her body, she'd either lost interest or lacked the energy to complete the second sleeve.

The abandoned project had languished in a corner of the family room for several months. I don't really know what prompted me to pick it up and decide to finish it for her in those last days, but it rather suddenly became an obsession. There was only one problem—I had no idea where in the pattern she'd left off. Solving the puzzle became a welcome diversion from the harsh reality of my mother's now rapid decline. And that afternoon, the day before she left us, I found the answer.

I found other answers too, over those final hours.

Nine days spent in a Hospice room—mildly tinged with the scent of antiseptic and peppermint and eerily quiet but for the soft whispers of families grieving as their loved ones slowly slipped away—had given me plenty of time to ponder my own situation. I was completely burned out—not so much from being my mother's sole caregiver until she'd entered Hospice care, but rather from the decades spent living a life that didn't feel genuinely mine.

My career was on the upswing—I held a senior management position at a respected non-profit organization; there was finally enough money to enjoy a few little luxuries. And I was miserable. I felt like an imposter, always afraid my colleagues would figure out that I wasn't "good enough" to sit in that corner office. I knew that in a few days' time, after Mum's funeral, I'd have to return to that life, and the thought filled me with dread.

Time stood still, it seemed, in those bittersweet, sunny December days. Carols played, and in the silent spaces between, a type of knowing slowly took hold of me. This, I realized, was a crossroads; a reckoning. A time to strip away the veneer of a life that didn't fit me and to embark on a quest for truth.

Growing up in England, my mother had always wanted to be a nurse. It was a desire so deeply-rooted that she still occasionally mentioned it, even at eighty-seven years of age. Her own mother, however, had had other plans for her, and at the tender age of fourteen, she'd been shipped off to secretarial school, denied the opportunity to obtain a secondary education. Mum wasn't allowed to leave the house with makeup on either—she'd "do her face" on the train heading into London each morning then wipe it off before arriving home in the evening.

Although she would never have said she'd lived an unhappy life, it certainly wasn't an authentic one. Living through the Blitz in her teen years, then coming to Canada in 1946 as a war bride with almost nothing, Mum's primary motivation had been the security of her family, accompanied by a healthy fear of scarcity and risk. It had never even occurred to her that perhaps she could make a fresh start in her new home, go back to school, and follow her dream. Instead, she had continued to follow the path that had been laid out for her. And as I watched her that afternoon, thin and frail, slowly slipping away from me, I felt deep in my bones that I did not want to repeat that pattern.

In her desire to protect me, Mum had managed, rather adeptly, to talk me out of pursuing my initial career choice. I had wanted to study English and Theatre—not to become a teacher, as everyone assumed, but rather, to be a working actor and a writer. Neither of those seemed a reliable, risk-free source of steady income, however, and my dear Mum had visions of me waiting tables and living on canned soup as I tried to make ends meet. While she wasn't about to repeat the mistakes her own mother had made—I was free to choose whatever course of study I wanted—the fear of lack was never far from the surface of our conversations, and it was clear to me that I should seek out a degree that would "pay the bills" and not leave me dependent on anyone else for my livelihood.

Above all, Mum wanted me to be safe—not an unreasonable desire for a parent. But the "safe" path is rarely, if ever, the most fulfilling one. Twenty-six years later, I had a business degree and a professional accounting designation on my office wall, a relatively high-paying job, and a very proud mother, but in my heart, barely a smoldering ember remained of the creative fire that had once burned within.

The thing about embers, though, is that they can be rekindled and catch fire once more, given the right environment…

It was incredibly difficult for me to imagine a life without my mother. She had been my best friend, my confidante, my sounding board, and my conscience. I had always sought her counsel, even in the last years of her life, and I a grown woman in my forties, Mum's opinion mattered greatly to me.

She had also been my knitting savior.

One of the worst experiences a novice knitter can have is dropping a stitch. It used to happen to me with some regularity, and Mum would always come to the rescue with her crochet hook and a smile. Five minutes later, all was well once more, and the work would be handed back, ready for me to go at it again.

Now, the tables had turned. I hadn't picked up a set of knitting needles for many years, but the work came back to me easily, like a long-absent friend, missed but never forgotten. The feel of the wool sliding through my fingers, the click-click of the needles, the pattern taking shape anew, somehow reminded me of a piece of my identity that I'd long ago abandoned.

As I proudly showed her the knitted sleeve, now an inch longer than before, her face took on a look of grace and peace I hadn't observed before. She could no longer speak, but in her eyes the message was clear: "Now I know you will be okay without me. You can figure out whatever challenges life presents to you. I can rest easy."

I felt that peace and grace as well. We spent the rest of the afternoon and early evening in comfortable silence, the King's College Choir Christmas CD playing softly in the background. As I worked the sleeve, I contemplated what was to come. After we said our final goodbyes, after the funeral, when the dust settled…who would I be? I didn't know. But I now knew who I wasn't—and I knew I could not return to that inauthentic life. I resolved to hand in my resignation at the first available opportunity. I was ready, I believed, to begin a new journey of self-discovery.

I got to the end of a row and paused for a moment. I was suddenly aware that the CD had stopped playing; and yet, I could still hear a choir singing softly. I couldn't locate the source of the sound—there were no carolers in the Hospice that afternoon, and the voices were faint and delicate, not emanating from the hallway. They were in the room—there was no mistaking it. Angels, serenading my mother as she prepared to go to her heavenly home.

Just after midnight, her struggle ended. I sat quietly with her for some minutes afterward, and those angelic voices appeared once again. This time, I felt certain, they were singing for *me*, letting me know I would not be alone as I stepped out into this new, authentic life.

As it turned out, though, I wasn't as ready to step into the unknown as I had at first thought.

The knitting having served its immediate purpose, I set it aside and turned my attention to the funeral, the winding up of my mother's estate, and working through my grief. I had planned to pick it up again once I had sorted out my path; but as so often happens, I became distracted. After a year's sabbatical, I talked myself back into a similar job (but convinced myself it was different because it carried less responsibility). Meanwhile, the knitting languished in a corner of my own family room—an ever-present reminder that I still was not listening to that inner voice.

Five years later, in the spring of 2016, I finally returned to it— struck by the idea of sending the cardigan to my mother's elder sister, Sylvia (by this time in her nineties and in an assisted living facility), so that she might have a piece of both my mother and me to treasure. I worked feverishly for several days, anxious to complete the work. As I boxed up the finished garment, lovingly adorned with a wide collar and brass buttons, I realized I was finally ready to let go of my mother—and my old identity. No angels serenaded me this time, but I still felt their presence, and thus began my search for a new career. The fear of change was gone.

As I walked back to my car after putting the box in the post, I thought back to that day in the Hospice when I'd first taken over the project. I smiled, feeling free at last.

"Look, Mum! I figured it out!"

ABOUT THE AUTHOR: Liz is a CPA with twenty years of experience in the charity and not-for-profit sectors, where her ability to distill complex financial information into understandable terms for people who hate numbers was highly prized. Realizing that accounting was not her authentic calling, she has leveraged this unique ability and pivoted into a new career as a trainer and coach in the health and performance arenas. Diagnosed at age seven with Celiac Disease, Liz has had a lifelong interest in the relationship between diet and overall health. She is an enthusiastic advocate of the primal lifestyle, aligning her clients' diet, habits, and lifestyle with the genetic makeup we still share with our paleolithic ancestors.

Liz Powell
Momentous Life Coaching
momentouslife.net
yourmomentouslife@gmail.com
905-938-1868

From Desperate Avoidance to Self Love

Loren Levitt

From a very young age I knew I was different. Outspoken and stubborn, I pushed all societal boundaries. It was as if I didn't speak the same language as other people. My parents divorced when I was one or two years old, and when my mother remarried, she and her new husband were gone most of the time, traveling abroad. Even when they were home, I felt like they were avoiding me. I felt alone, isolated, different, and unlovable. It was a feeling I would carry with me for a long time.

I started having trouble in school and was sent to a psychologist and various tutors; I also took multiple tests for learning disabilities and started to believe there was not only something wrong with me, but that I might not be very smart as well.

When I reached high school age, my parents suggested I go to a boarding school in Colorado specifically designed for students with learning disabilities and other "behavioral issues." It was like being freed from prison! I could breathe again, and as if by magic, I fit right in with the other students. This was also the time when I was introduced to alcohol and other substances. I didn't particularly like the taste of alcohol at first. But I soon realized that after a couple of drinks, I felt this overwhelming sense that I was okay! I became prettier, smarter, funnier, and felt no insecurities whatsoever. Ahhh, this was what I've been waiting for! A real Eureka moment, where everything falls into place. I wished I always felt like this!

My love of school—especially the drinking—continued into

college. Everything seemed fine, until my sophomore year, when I began having strange, frightening symptoms—heart palpitations and difficulty breathing, accompanied by fears of public places and crowds. I even had visions of being trapped in classrooms. I had no idea what this was or why it was happening. I told friends about the symptoms but no one seemed to understand.

"You mean like stage fright?" they'd ask, "Everyone gets that."

"No... I mean, yes, that feeling, but all the time..."

Once again, I felt something was terribly wrong with me, and drinking was the only "medication" that helped.

Unfortunately, my medicine of choice brought with it a whole lot of shame. When I drank I became belligerent, only to forget my behavior the next day. I would wake up in different locations, usually at a friend's or a guy's house, and often in a pool of my own urine. It was so humiliating! Hungover, anxious, terrified, and filled with shame that I had done it again, I would lay there, motionless, wondering if anyone knew what had happened. Could I try to cover it up? I would sometimes flip over the mattress and was even more horrified if it had leaked through. If it did, I would try to leave undetected and pray I never saw that person again. I hated how I felt and who I was, yet I couldn't seem to stop.

During my college years I also became somewhat of a vagabond. I began at Drury College in Missouri, then worked at Club Med before enrolling in the Friends World Program (now called Global University) of Long Island University. Through that program I returned to London, where I'd lived for a time while with Drury, then to the other places including Boston, Houston, back to Colorado, and then California, where I would live for eight years.

When I went into my first rehab I knew I wasn't ready to quit drinking but I thought maybe I could find a way to cut back. They said I was a "problem drinker," which meant I wasn't that bad, right? I kept moving around, working odd jobs until they started to get in the way of my drinking. Truth is, I rarely wanted to leave the house, except of course to buy alcohol. I spent most of my time on the couch, often losing track of time, sometimes not even knowing if it was day or night. I grew sicker and sicker, more anxious, and agoraphobic. I began to hope I'd simply drink myself to death and it would all be over.

There was one day that stands out in my mind. It started out the same as every other—with me sitting on my porch of my Laguna Beach home after waking up with the shakes. Then, as soon it was opening time, I set out on my daily walk of shame to the liquor store a couple of blocks away. I bought a handle of vodka, a liter of diet Seven-Up and two boxes of cigarettes. I remember they would always wrap everything in a brown bag then put it into a black plastic bag—their attempt to be discreet. But it was a pretty small town, and I would keep my head down, hoping no one I knew would see me or stop to talk. I knew what I looked like—red-faced, shaking, and dripping with sweat. I wore baggy clothes because I had gained a lot of weight. The whole way home my focus was in getting back to the safety of my porch as fast as possible. I knew what was in that bag would help me to forget even going to the store in the first place.

I made my first drink and lit my cigarette, already anticipating the cloud of unconsciousness I would soon drift to. But that day, instead of that delicious feeling of warmth going down my throat then spreading to my whole body, I began throwing up and dry heaving. I couldn't keep it down. *Please stay down.* I literally throbbed for it. I became hysterical, thinking I might not get the relief I so desperately needed and terrified I'd have a seizure, which had happened before when I tried to detox on my own. With steely determination, I kept drinking and eventually got a couple of big gulps down. But I remember thinking, what if alcohol doesn't work anymore? Could I ever learn to live without it? All my previous attempts at quitting had been half-hearted, but that day, for the first time, I had a glimpse of wonder—there was a possibility of something different.

The night before entering my last treatment, I drank so much that

I fell onto a chair. The next day I woke up with bloody knees and a black eye; I had also pissed in the pants I'd been wearing for the better part of a week. This, on top of my typical booze-plus-cigarette stench.

I left for detox with nothing but my toothbrush. No suitcase, no clean change of clothes, not even a hairbrush. I guess I knew that none of that would matter. THIS is what it looked like! I had nothing left to prove!

After my detox week I went back into a treatment facility. I found I wasn't scared or even nervous—that's how many times I had done this; in fact, being there felt safe and familiar. Nothing I experienced was any different than any other time. But I was different. I had become willing—to be honest, to be vulnerable, and, most importantly, to take in new information. I actually listened to others and what worked for them. I had always tried to rationalize my way out of everything. I was so analytical and in my head because it felt safer there. I had built up a façade, like I had it all together. I lied, I manipulated, and could play the court jester all day long, as long as you didn't ask me to be real. I didn't have the first clue as to what that meant. Even the thought was terrifying.

Getting sober wasn't the problem; it was staying sober. Alcohol had become my best friend and confidant, and without it I had no idea who I was. What if I began scratching the surface, trying to find any part of humanity, only to find there was nothing salvageable left?

Once I left the last treatment facility, I vowed to do anything and everything I was told to do. Though this was against every stubborn obstinate fiber of my being, I knew if I continued to think and behave as I did before, I would be right back where I was, shaking on my porch or worse. I was going to have to re-learn from the ground up. I would have to strip away every layer of masks and falsehoods I had so dearly held onto. There was no more victim, no one else to blame. This would be the beginning of a new life for me!

I had been so thirsty for so long—not for alcohol, but for Love. Self love. I didn't even know what that meant. Now, I slowly began to learn. None of this was an easy or smooth process for me. It took nearly a year before I felt the least bit comfortable in my own skin. It took me years to learn how to really tell the truth. Not just to others, but to myself. I joined a women's AA group which I loved and actually looked forward to going to. They embraced me scared, anxious, and practically crawling when I first came in. We didn't always talk about drinking, we talked about life. How to live life. I found I actually wanted to be accountable.

Before joining that group, I used to think the big book, AA, and the steps were all some kind of weird clique or Christian cult. My sponsor helped me understand more about them—how they originated and the purpose of each step—recognizing there is a problem (which, in my case, was itself a BIG problem); learning to release the fear and shame of our past and what we've done; taking responsibility; and becoming honest. And, in time, finding a Higher Power.

One day, I headed to a small coffee shop near my house to write down one of my steps. As I sat at an outside table, looking out over the ocean, I started flashing back to all the things I've been through, and how many times I could have died or was seriously in harm's way. Suddenly I realized, for the very first time, that I was not alone. So many times I had cursed God and the Universe for turning me into the monster I was, yet now I saw there was a reason for everything. I had been protected this whole time. This had not been the curse I believed, but a miracle that I needed to share and pass on to others. I felt my shoulders drop, the wind and salty air on my face, and realized this world was no longer something to conquer on my own, I was part of something much, much bigger.

Soon after, I began working in an inpatient treatment facility and eventually became an addiction counselor. Over the many years I worked there, I found that the more honest, vulnerable, and raw I could be with others about my journey, the more empowered they were to be open to healing. I had finally found my sense of purpose!

Today, with years of sobriety under my belt, I live in a beautiful place in the mountains of Colorado with my amazingly supportive husband and two dogs. I have a life coaching private practice and also work with people around personal training and nutrition. It is no longer about who I was, but who I've become. I still go to AA meetings, sponsor other women, and belong to a number of other women's groups. Life is still unraveling in layers like an onion. I learn more about myself all the time—some things are interesting, others painful, but all bring me to even deeper levels of love. Miracles do happen, if only you're willing to wait, watch, and listen.

ABOUT THE AUTHOR: Loren Levitt was born in Houston, Texas. After attending boarding school in Colorado, she went to Long Island University. Through their global program for experiential learning, she lived and worked with various indigenous groups in India, Central America, and Peru and graduated with a BA in International Relations. After years of dedication to her own personal and spiritual growth, Loren received her certification in Addiction Counseling, and later an M.A. in Counseling Psychology. Loren lives in Colorado with her husband, where she maintains a private practice in Life Coaching and Counseling. She is currently working on a book dedicated to personal growth and empowered living.

Loren D Levitt
Levitt Life Coaching
levittlifecoaching.com
Loren@levittlifecoaching.com
720-468-7186

Open Mind, Open Heart
Beth Lopez

I'm an avid walker, and I usually prefer walking by myself. I breathe the fresh air while I contemplate and meditate. But one afternoon, when my husband was at the tail end of a cold and not feeling up to going to the gym, something nudged me to invite him on my walk, and he agreed.

As we began walking, a voice whispered in my ear to come clean with him. I wanted to ignore the advice, but the voice kept getting louder. I was told to "confess" to him about the double life I'd been leading. The new year loomed, and I suddenly realized that I didn't want to enter 2019 in hiding from my husband, or the world.

While we walked along, our feet crunching over dried leaves, I took a deep breath and grappled with how I would let the words flow so that he'd have understanding and compassion for what I do and why. Finally, I felt ready to speak.

"I have something to tell you," I said, "I want you to know who I work with in my business—who my clients are."

I explained that when I started working with healing energy and clients in 2015, I had made a conscious decision not to work in the Los Angeles area because I didn't want to serve people with more liberal lifestyles and views than mine, given my Mormon background. For that reason, I had decided to narrow my range to Orange County, an area I viewed as more conservative, and within my "safe zone."

My husband listened intently. In January of that same year he had chosen to become baptized in the Mormon faith, and he had done it for me.

"I've discovered over the last three years that the Universe has a funny way of teaching you the lessons you came here to learn," I told him. I went on to explain that the clientele I'd been trying to stay away from was the gay community, which is more prevalent in the Los Angeles area. Despite my efforts to steer clear of homosexual clients, they had begun to find me online—lesbian women in particular. My business had become sixty percent gay women, and they continued to refer many new clients to me!

I also revealed that I found it necessary to spend quite a few sessions with my own energy healer to release the negative feelings surrounding this phenomenon. Most of the feelings and beliefs surrounding homosexuality I'd inherited from my father, a devout Mormon.

It All Started with a Hug

I have never been what you would call a "hugger," but it was a hug back in October 2013 that sparked my spiritual awakening and completely changed my life. A coworker had gone on vacation, and though I didn't know where, I noticed that upon her return she radiated a happy, loving energy. This energy was so strong and peaceful that I asked for a hug. I am so glad that I did! Later I discovered that she'd gone on a spiritual retreat to Italy and spent a great deal of time meditating on the grounds of St. Francis of Assisi. Through that embrace, she had transmitted his energy to me.

Over the next two months I would experience profound shifts of the heart and mind. At the time, I had a job that was high-paying but no longer fed my soul. In fact, it chipped away at my very being as I struggled with office politics and racial prejudices that dictated who climbed the corporate ladder and who remained stagnant. I'd grown weary of proving my worth to the company again and again. The awakening sparked by the hug showed me that I had given my job so much power that I lost my zest for life and my sense of self. I knew it was time for some changes.

Enlightened Directly Through Jesus

By January 2014, I felt Jesus in my heart as clearly as if He had spoken to me. I suddenly had a thirst to know anything and everything about Him. At the time, I was not actively involved in the Mormon Church, though I'd belonged to the religion since birth and was baptized at age eight. My awakening caused me to want to go back to the church, but I wasn't living what would be considered a suitable life by its standards. I'd been divorced and was in a relationship with my present husband, but not yet married. My desire to return to church on the right terms served as a catalyst for making our relationship official. After we married, my husband got baptized in the church, as did my twelve-year-old child.

At first, I was flying high! I thought I had figured it all out and was right where I needed to be. I quit my job and began helping clients with healing energy. However, after about six months, I realized that the energy work I was called to do—and clients I was attracting—were diametrically opposed to the church. The religion that had been with me all of my life and served as my spiritual foundation only believes in heterosexual marriage. Living otherwise brings condemnation. That's when my double life began.

Things came to a head in 2018. I had been struggling all year to live as a devout Mormon while at the same time serving more and more gay clients. During this time, I did a lot of soul searching and meditating. What I discovered was that we are all one. There truly is no separation between any of us. We all came from the same source, we all carry the energy of the same source, and we are all here on this life journey to encourage and enhance our soul evolvement and development.

During that walk, I told my husband all of this. I told him that I had come to the conclusion that I would neither judge nor refuse to work with someone based on their life choices, no matter how different they were from my own.

Finally, I told him that I realized what I was doing didn't align with the church, but I vowed to let Jesus keep leading and teaching me as I worked to heal those who come to me for help.

As we approached our home, I wondered how my husband would

react; after all, he had followed me into this church and as far as I knew had accepted its doctrines. Imagine my joy and relief when he said he felt enlightened by my confession and that I should continue to do what I had been called to do. My heart was so happy he understood that it wasn't about me, but about my clients. I have been led to help those who may otherwise be shunned, labeled outcasts, or discriminated against.

"Coming Clean" with Mom

The confession to my husband opened me up to speak to my mother, which considering my upbringing was no easy endeavor. My parents had always followed the church's teachings and rules. They also worked hard to keep me on the church's path.

When I was growing up, my father forbade me from going to sleepovers with other girls for fear that I would become a lesbian. My first marriage was to a Mormon boy because my parents didn't want me to date or marry outside the faith. Even years later, when I stayed with a girlfriend after leaving my husband, my father accused me of being gay. Needless to say, my stomach was in knots at the mere thought of telling my mother the truth about my work, but I knew it was something I had to do.

Finally, the day arrived. Like with my husband, I held nothing back. I told Mom that more than half of my clients were lesbians and that I had recently travelled to Spokane, Washington to certify my clients, all of whom were lesbians, to do the healing work that I did. I also explained how many people I helped and how many of them had worked with me for more than a year. She and my father had done a really good job of giving me a firm foundation, I said, but now, in order to be true to my authentic self, I needed to leave the teachings of the church behind.

After listening quietly to everything I had to say, Mom responded with a confession of her own: years earlier she had been employed by lesbians and found them to be very nice people. Then she really shocked me by saying that if I had my own personal relationship with Jesus and didn't need the church anymore, I should follow my heart and leave.

I assured her that this was the case. I had learned what I needed to learn from church, which was servitude, and now I was using those lessons to serve my tribe/soul family.

Shortly after my confession, my husband announced that he had something important to say: he felt we should leave the church.

"Yes, oh, my goodness, yes," I responded. "Let's do it!"

"I'm not talking about just becoming inactive," he said, "I'm talking about officially leaving the church."

I gulped. "I know. Let's do it."

He said, "I feel leaving the church will allow you to spread your message, and you'll be able to work more freely because you won't be worrying about being found out. This way you can serve whoever you are called to serve."

Two weeks went by, and then I got another nudge to fill out the paperwork and submit it so that we could officially be released. My husband and I wrote a letter to the head bishop and sent it.

Here we go, I thought. Another enormous life change for me and my family!

Waves of Grief

As happy as I was to be free of the constraints of the Mormon religion, I was conflicted. In many ways I loved the church and the firm religious foundation it had instilled in me. Even so, I was blindsided when—boom!—the grief came rushing in. This grief literally tore up the foundation upon which my entire life was built. Back to my healer I went in attempt to understand what was happening.

I soon discovered that when you purge old parts of your life that no longer serve you, you also let go of what you once believed. There is a grief in letting go of those old beliefs, and it's a normal, human reaction. Whether those old beliefs were good or bad for me was irrelevant; they had been deeply engrained in me practically since birth. When they were removed, there was a void that had to be mourned and healing that had to be done.

In the process of grieving, I found and met my true self. I uncovered what *Beth* really believes in and the contributions she wishes to offer the world. I found that I had to learn to stand on my own two feet, upright from the core of my very being, and embody this new transition in my life. I had to learn to live my own life according to my own principles.

Finding Awareness

During this process, I came to realize why I've been called to coach lesbian woman. They too have struggled to define themselves in a world that all too often seeks to pigeonhole and categorize them in a way that does not reflect who they really are. Today I am honored to know that I have discovered my soul purpose and that I can wholeheartedly help others discover their authentic selves through their inner greatness so they can pursue their goals and dreams.

ABOUT THE AUTHOR: Beth Lopez is a Master Energy Healer and Transformational leader who incorporates Christ Consciousness into her healing sessions. She is a certified ThetaHealer®, Usui Reiki Master and Teacher, Astrologist, Numerologist, Fairy Lightworker, and Angel Light worker. She also has certifications in the Akashic Records and Crystal Reiki. Beth's Rainbow Pathway Process helps clients heal the ego and subconscious, live more from the heart, become their master selves, and step into their soul calling with power, expression, and an abundant mindset. Through her Soulistic Business Program she helps others with a spiritual calling share themselves and their message with the world. Beth works with women, primarily those in the LGBT community.

Beth Lopez
Souls Awakening Academy
universalsoulcoach.com
universalsoulcoach@gmail.com
818-653-8262

The Flower and The Butterfly
Michele Weisman

In nature, the relationship between the flower and the butterfly exemplifies the most ideal form of symbiosis. Rooted in Mother Earth, the flower nurtures and offers connection from a fixed place. With its intoxicating scent, it draws the butterfly in and invites it to partake of its sweet, fortifying nectar. The butterfly is free and untethered, yet it also nurtures and offers connection by pollinating the flower. The flower's future thus assured, and the butterfly, true to its nature, takes to the breeze.

The same can be said of people—the "flowers" prefer and provide stability from the home base, while the "butterflies" yearn for freedom and new adventures. Their relationship is also a dance of symbiosis and balance. Authenticity is knowing which one we are and living from that place. My epiphany that I am the butterfly and not the flower was exhilarating and transformative; it forever separated my life into a Before and After. In that blessed moment I understood the *why* behind so many questions, all related to the something's-not-right feeling in my chest, the tension in my fingers, and that edge in my personality.

I had often felt not-right, and though I lacked any spiritual insights at the time, I sensed that I wasn't living my soul's purpose. This knowing didn't make me feel better; in fact, it made me feel worse. I felt guilty that my beautiful family and home weren't enough for me, but the truth was that they *weren't*, at least, not all the time. I loved being a mother, and the immense satisfaction I derived from nurturing my two daughters often filled me up enough. For a while. Then the satisfaction would ultimately leak out again, leaving me deflated and wanting.

At these times, I often thought about traveling. I had never stopped yearning for another unhurried, unscripted adventure like I had when I was twenty-two. Those seven weeks backpacking through Europe after college was the most freeing, the most fun, the most "me" experience I had ever had. It called to me many times while I lived the mom life in the suburbs of Long Island, reaching a crescendo as I enviously watched each of my girls leave for their study abroad semesters.

Facing an empty nest and the rest of my life without a clear purpose or direct means of fulfillment brought me to a painfully low emotional setpoint. The silver lining of my volatile mix of dissatisfaction, envy, and self-denial was that it created a perfect storm, prompting a fresh round of introspection. What started with "I wish *I* could study abroad!" morphed into "*Why* can't I study abroad?", and finally, "Why *can't* I study abroad?".

I found myself convincing, especially when I considered my final point—I had always wanted to be fluent in Spanish. It was my minor in college, and my parents had denied my request to study abroad. Teenage angst and self-importance renewed, I googled "immersive Spanish language program overseas adult." All I needed now was permission. The girls were both out of the house. I had met my primary responsibility as a mother, and I knew I was close to a breaking point. Permission granted. My heart thumped with a mix of excitement and fear as I pulled out my Visa and clicked on "Submit" from my kitchen, enrolling in an immersive Spanish language program. For four weeks. In Costa Rica. By myself.

I was less convinced of my sound decision-making the night before I left. Struggling to shove the pile of mosquito repellant sprays and wipes—purchased each of the three times I shopped at REI—into my already overweight suitcase, I second-guessed my judgment. Panicking slightly, I even considered the possibility that I didn't truly want to go but was drawn to the challenge of proving to myself and my family that I could do it.

On April 16, 2016, just shy of my fifty-fifth birthday I flew to San José. I had chosen to spend the first three weeks of the program in Heredia, a small, quaint colonial city about forty minutes northwest of the capital, and the last week on the school's beach location in Sámara, a lowkey, bohemian-vibed town in the Guanacaste region.

The first morning of classes, I arrived at the brightly painted stuccoed building, feeling like most students on the first day of school—excited with a tinge of nausea. Once inside, I slowly assessed the decision I had made four months and three thousand, nine hundred and eighty-four miles earlier. There, exchanging "where are you froms" and "how long are you stayings" were a mix of early twentysomethings and a few very slightly older girls (I want to say "women" but, honestly, they were girls).

By the end of the day, I had made my first friend. Ghina lived in Canada, having moved from Tunisia several years earlier. She was in her early thirties and Spanish would be her fourth language. We agreed to speak to each other in English, and I relaxed into the comfort of knowing I was indeed correct to have given myself this timeout from suburban wife…I mean *life*. Though self-doubt and its sidekick guilt—both staples of motherhood—had accompanied me on the plane, they were fading fast, and satisfaction and relief were stepping in.

In getting to know Ghina and the other students, I recognized that I was amongst fellow adventurers, learners, and free spirits. The initial shock of the age difference wore off as well, and I soon settled into a comfortable pace, like the in-and-out rhythm of breath during a good night's sleep. Our schedules Monday through Friday were devoted to learning, but ended early enough so we could enjoy a cooking, dance, or yoga class. Each Friday, I eagerly participated in the optional weekend excursion to revel in the natural beauty a few hours outside the city.

My second weekend there, I, along with three girls from Germany and an American medical student named Adrienne, signed up to explore the region surrounding Rincón de la Vieja National Park. Activities were to include ziplining over the lush canopy of the rainforest, horseback riding and soaking in the hot mineral springs. I skipped the horseback riding, but did everything else, including ignoring my better judgment in climbing a slippery waterfall. I also climbed down the bank of the waterfall after deciding not to jump, which in retrospect, would have been easier and safer.

The German girls—Francesca, Nadja, and Lena—had been struggling with their Spanish, so they spoke German to each other whenever they could. After breakfast I grabbed my cup of coffee and got up from the table, thinking I would free them from their obligation of speaking to me in Spanish, or English, which they all spoke well. Holding a cup of coffee, like a glass of wine, always makes me feel purposeful and comfortable; as in "I'm not alone; I have a cup of coffee." It was an unhurried morning, and I strolled past the dining pavilion to look at one of the many clusters of muted yellow hibiscus bordering the walkways.

The sky was overcast and though I didn't feel even the slightest breeze, I noticed the hibiscus moving back and forth. Curious, I moved slightly closer until my eyes noticed a yellow butterfly flitting about the yellow hibiscus. The butterfly seemed to appear and then disappear each time its graceful wings became camouflaged against the outer edges of the petals. I had to focus to keep from losing sight of it. The moments when I lost sight were like the gaps between thoughts during meditation. And like the ease which comes when resistant thought ceases, wisdom quietly crept in.

Sucking in my breath as my brain caught up with the message my soul had already synthesized, I understood the lesson the Universe was showing me.

"I'm *not* the flower, I'm the *butterfly*!!!"

Relief washed over me as my epiphany delivered waves of fresh clarity. I kept repeating it out loud, "I'm the *butterfly*; I'm the *butterfly*;

I'm the *butterfly*." Each time I said it with a slightly different, slightly deeper level of understanding. I finally comprehended that I had been the victim of mistaken identity. Flowers are rooted, butterflies are free; that's why I had been feeling so stuck and so unfulfilled.

My husband Paul almost never calls me by my name, Michele. He calls me Flower. To him, I am beautiful, and somewhat delicate. The sweetness of this term of endearment had always made me feel cared for and beloved. Knowing he said it with the purest of intentions, I accepted it, signing my notes, cards, and emails to him either with the word or my simple drawing of petals around a dot, and two curved lines for the stem and the leaves. I was wise to choose a spouse very much like my father—a kind, generous, dependable, traditional family man.

I, however, am not traditional. I prefer adventure, spontaneity, change, excitement, and movement. Yet I acquiesced to the predictable, homogenous, stable suburban lifestyle of the last twenty-one years, not only forfeiting my carefree, free-spirited essence but burying it. And almost forgetting it.

My connection to butterflies had actually begun two years earlier, when a monarch landed on a chair next to mine as I rested in my backyard. It wasn't the landing that drew my attention, but the staying. Recovering from a bad bike fall, I was emotionally and physically dejected, and this butterfly's unusual behavior made me wonder. I even spoke to it, sensing that it could've been a loved one wanting to lift my spirits.

I returned home from Costa Rica enlivened and refreshed, and though not perfectly fluent in Spanish, pretty close. Enlightened with the lesson the Universe had shared with me, I was intent on finding ways to incorporate my learning into my life. As it turns out, the wisdom in this lesson is still revealing itself to me, just as butterflies continue to fly and land in my path.

Reconnecting with my love of travel allowed me to reconnect with my free-spirited nature, which I had been estranged from by my beliefs—my beliefs about what I, as a mother could and couldn't be and do. Denying parts of myself for so long was so much work—dissatisfying, unfulfilling, soul-sucking work. Answering the parts of myself that were calling for me to come play moved me in the direction of flow and ease.

Authenticity looks like being brave or courageous but, really, it's what's easier. Pretending that everything is great while consistently meeting others' expectations is what's hard.

I will always love my husband's sweet term of endearment for me, just as I will always cherish the years I was happily rooted in family life. But I will never again deny who I know I am.

ABOUT THE AUTHOR: Michele is a writer, adventurer, and owner of Mome Coaching, a practice that focuses on guiding mothers in releasing whatever is holding them back from truly loving their lives. Though moms are her "sweet spot," Michele loves bringing inspiration, connection, and empowerment to all seeking clarity and healing. Prior to coaching, she founded and directed a recruiting business that served the financial technology industry for fourteen years. Throughout her life, Michele has derived tremendous fulfillment as a volunteer and advocate for hunger relief, homelessness, and animal welfare and rescue. When she's not working, she enjoys spending time with her family and speaking Spanish every chance she gets.

Michele Weisman, CPC, Transformation Life Coach
Individual coaching and group workshops
Release – Reimagine – Rediscover Your True Self
momecoaching.com ~ 516-210-6518
@momeoaching on Instagram and Facebook

Inner Authenticity, Outer Beauty
Anne Marie Foley

We are constantly being molded by our experiences, both painful and joyful, large and seemingly insignificant. Many, many things molded me along my journey, but it was my first deep spiritual awakening at the age of twenty-three that irrevocably changed me and made me tune in to the intuitive gifts that until that point I had been afraid to acknowledge.

It was Christmastime, and I had just returned to the States after a trip to Ireland to visit my family. My plane had no sooner touched down on the runway when I became extremely ill. It took a few trips to the ER before I received a diagnosis: meningitis. There had been an outbreak of the disease in Ireland and I had somehow contracted it.

My body was wracked with pain; pain so severe I could barely think. All I knew was that I desperately wanted it to end. I spent much of those days praying the rosary and crying. One day the nurse came in to hook up a new IV with yet another antibiotic. She saw me praying and said, "I pray this works for you, sweet angel." She then asked me if I would like to see a priest and, with tears flowing down my cheeks, I told her yes. When the chaplain arrived he prayed over me and administered last rights. *Maybe*, I thought, *my time on earth really has come to an end.*

Suddenly the room was enveloped in a fog. I looked up and saw the chaplain gently float away, then felt my own spirit raise out of my body. The brightest white light I had ever seen filled the space, and I heard a female voice gently whisper, "Not now, dear, you have work to do." I then floated, light as a feather, back down into my body. I didn't know how much time had passed but I was being taken down for another MRI. I was wearing a fresh gown, a cap had been placed on my head, and, as this MRI was to be taken with contrast, another IV was inserted into my skin. When we got into the elevator, two old ladies were already in there.

"She looks like an Angel," one of them said, "Can we touch her?"

As they placed their hands on me I felt such a beautiful warm heat emanating from both of them. I looked up and smiled and said, "Thank you!" More tears flowed then, but they were different from those I had cried earlier. The excruciating pain was subsiding; I was starting to feel my body again.

Three weeks later I left the hospital a completely different person from the one who went in. My experience had left me with a knowing that a greater power existed. Not only did I no longer fear death, I knew that I had a responsibility to that divine power to really live my life, not just go through the motions.

I was engaged at the time, and after a lengthy recovery I regained my health and started planning my wedding, which was to take place in Ireland. As I went about dealing with the thousands of details associated with such an affair, I realized there was an uneasiness somewhere deep down in my soul. I loved this man; he came from an amazing family, and I knew I would have a beautiful life with him, yet I couldn't help but wonder whether I was making the right choice.

I pushed the feeling aside and on January 17, 1998, we got married. I had no idea what lay ahead of me, which was actually a blessing in disguise. Had I known, I might not have had the two beautiful children which have made this whole journey worth it. Giving birth was another truly miraculous experience that forever changed me, for I realized for the first time that I had the ability to love uncondi-tionally. I learned what the heart is capable of.

My second big awakening came fourteen years later, when my marriage came to an end. This event didn't just rock my world, it ripped it out from under me. Being born and raised in Ireland, and from a Catholic family, the decision to divorce was probably the most difficult I'd ever had to make. Eventually I would come to realize that divorce is like a death; however, it is also a chance for rebirth, an opportunity to be honest with your authentic self.

Of course, this did not make it any easier to deal with at the time. Though I knew both parties must accept responsibility when their marriage doesn't work out, I found myself on my bedroom floor crying from the deepest place in my soul. Had the life I'd lived for all these years been a lie? Had I betrayed my own soul by not listening to its warning, or was this all part of my journey? This led to me to ask things like, is this journey already written and we are just walking it? I had plenty of questions, but no answers.

Towards the end of the divorce proceedings, I went to the dentist for a regular routine filling and it went terribly wrong. I was overdosed on novocaine and my lingual nerve was severed, which left me with a permanent injury and living with chronic nerve pain. I had no idea that this would be my biggest awakening, through which I would be guided to tools and modalities that would change my life.

At the time I was working in nutraceutical sales and was coming across some very inspiring people, from pro athletes to gifted healers to people who'd had organ transplants or due to some other life-altering event found themselves having to start over. Listening to their stories, it was clear to me that I was being put on a different path, but what? I was still living with a tremendous amount of pain on a daily basis and had no idea what to do about it. One day I was challenged with a question: *What are you doing to help yourself heal?*

I didn't have an answer. That question had hit a place so deep in my soul, maybe because for the first time I had come across someone who could see all the pain I was doing such a great job of managing.

In the days that followed I found a local yoga studio and took my first class. As the teacher guided us through the various poses, I felt like I had finally come home. I then started to take meditation classes and meditate every day. I quickly fell in love with this practice because it made me feel connected to Source and have a deep sense of peace I had never experienced before.

It was in the midst of all this pain that I started to be me. Working in the beauty and esthetic industry, I had dealt with people—mostly women—who were seeking external beauty. Now, through my yoga and meditation practice, I started to realize that to be truly beautiful, you had to be your most authentic self; that there was a power in being vulnerable and true; and that there was a freedom attached to all of this. I decided I wanted to teach others that beauty had to come from within in order to manifest on the outside.

Around this time, I also decided to take Reiki, which I had been drawn to since I was child but never pursued. Through yet another divine appointment, I found an amazing Master teacher. Once again, I had that feeling of home when I began to practice. Reiki became a vehicle for my intuitive gifts. I started to see a big pattern, and the more I started to trust the journey the more God placed beautiful, authentic people into my life, preparing me for my healing work, and guiding me all the way. All I had to do was release my fear, show up, and listen to my intuition. I noticed a pattern here too, for whenever I listened to that intuition I always ended up exactly where I was supposed to be.

I started to help others, not only through the laying of hands but in sharing the knowledge and wisdom that had assisted me. As I got deeper into the work I started attracting a lot of mothers, people going through a divorce, and others who found themselves having to start life over. In sharing my own journey, I was teaching people how to trust and surrender to the process. In showing my own vulnerability, I was empowering others to do the same. A healer doesn't claim to actually heal others; we simply hold the space, thereby allowing them to tap into their own healing and intuitive sense.

I also continued my esthetic work, as this was still an excellent way for me to reach people who were seeking to be more themselves. The more engaged I became with listening to their stories, the more I was able to intuitively pick up on where their wound was and how I could help them. The desire to be more beautiful nearly always stems from some trauma and/or conditioned thoughts and behavior one is exposed to during the formative years. These thoughts, emotions, and behaviors have often attached themselves to the subconscious.

After so many years of searching, I knew I had found my calling: to help others heal these wounds, learn to trust themselves so they may trust others, and figure out who they really are and authentically live from that space.

The journey of life is not an easy one; we all are tested one way or another through trauma and pain, death and divorce, or some other experience. Through these tests—and with the unconditional love and support of my parents, Pauline and Vincent Foley—I have learned how resilient my own spirit is, yet I am constantly overwhelmed by the resiliency of my clients. Along my journey I have also met the most incredible people who have either changed me or helped me to be a more authentically beautiful me. My mission, in my healing work and in sharing my story here, is to help others become their most authentic selves.

Don't be afraid of the power that exists in you; don't be swayed by the naysayers. Instead, follow your heart, for it will lead you home to the most beautiful authentic place. If you find that life is forcing you to start over, please don't be afraid; seek out the help and support you need. Start to meditate; find the practice of yoga, eat healthy, and honor your body. Learn how powerful it is when you connect the mind, body, and spirit. Know you are more powerful when you are authentically beautiful!

ABOUT THE AUTHOR: Anne Marie is an intuitive counselor, Reiki Master, beauty consultant, and owner of "Healing with Me," a practice committed to holistic wellbeing. Born and raised in beautiful Limerick, Ireland, she emigrated to the U.S. in 1996 and settled on Long Island. Anne Marie studied marketing and accounting, then Esthetics and makeup, but after a series of spiritual awakenings including a near-death experience, a painful divorce, and a permanent injury to her lingual nerve, her natural intuitive gifts emerged and took her on another path. Today, Anne Marie uses her psychic abilities and Reiki to help others heal from traumas and become beautiful from the inside out.

Anne Marie Foley
Healing with Me!
annemariefoley.com
amfoley@yahoo.com
631-764-1989

My Awakening to Change It Up!

Nina Antinora

It's funny, when thinking back on what authenticity meant to me twenty or even ten years ago, and now contributing to a book about the "beauty of authenticity"—I realize that before my transformation I never would have associated beauty with authenticity. In fact, when thinking about my truth and living an authentic life on my terms, the words and feelings that came up were fear, anxiety, and utter confusion.

Yet here I am today, not only embracing but celebrating and revealing my true self on a daily basis to help inspire others to live a life filled with joy, grace, and purpose. It has been a journey filled with the ups and downs, of great love and loss, triumphs, uncertainty, growth, and eventually the aha moment that allowed me to finally dropkick fear in the face.

Let me take you back to the moment when my life forever changed. It was the spring of 2002. My beautiful mother Suzanne was being treated for cancer. We were told it was limited small-cell lung cancer and that it had not spread. So we fought—HARD.

I took a sabbatical from my career in TV to be by her side. I accompanied her to all appointments—from chemo and radiation to new consults, meetings with holistic practitioners, and twenty-one blood transfusions. I even managed to get her in to see a world-renowned holistic miracle man who accepted my mom into a clinical trial in Germany. All we needed was the approval from her oncologist. During the entire process, I made it my number one mission to save my mother's life. She was only fifty. This wasn't going to be the end, not on my watch.

However, God (the Universe or whatever you may believe in) had other plans. My entire world came crashing down when the doctor broke the news. The cancer must have been hiding out all along and had now spread to her bones and brain. There was nothing more they could do. My selfless mother's initial reaction was to look at me and say "I'm sorry. I am so sorry I won't be there. I am sorry I am going to leave you." It was one of those surreal (out of body) moments. An insufferable moment that is impossible to forget.

After losing my amazing mom the fall of 2002, I realized that you can have life goals but you can't control the outcomes. What was meant to be will be. Yet, though I knew this I had no clue how to release the control button. I had to figure out the best way to pick up the pieces and move forward. But how? Living a life without my mom felt impossible. She'd been my best friend, my biggest support system, and my greatest inspiration. She was one badass, smart, and strong woman with the largest empathic heart.

I was twenty-seven years old and really wanted to make life changes; however, I lacked the tools and—without my mom—the support system or beliefs needed to overcome my fears.

I figured the only way to cope with the gigantic hole in my heart was to throw myself into my work. I was a hardcore East Coast executive producer living in north Jersey, working in Manhattan, and producing events around the world. Go. Go. Go. I was extremely type-A and was fondly known among my colleagues as "Clipboard Nina." It was all I really had (or so I thought at the time). It boosted my confidence, gave me a huge sense of pride, purpose, and, to be honest, defined me. So, I forged ahead and piled on more and more responsibility; I also kept a full social calendar. Anything that made me sad or required me to tap into my fears or self-doubt was pushed aside. This also meant pushing down my sensitive, emotional, and spiritual side. The side of me that is tethered to my mom, my soul, and my life's greater purpose.

My definition of success was also based on very different things back then. Mostly, it had to do with "keeping up with the Joneses"—a very fear-based and learned behavior I now realize wasn't aligned with how I truly felt inside. This unconscious misalignment was the source of my stress and anxiety; however, without my mom's support I was too afraid of what other people would think if I floated left instead of charging right. Although I was extremely confident and a well-respected leader in business, my personal life suffered (secretly) due to me constantly second-guessing myself. To stray from the status quo and pursue my own passions, deep desires, and what felt right inside was way too scary.

It was much easier to focus on the tangible, socially acceptable brand of success: surplus of funds in my bank account, driving my Porsche, owning my first home at a young age, even dating men that fit someone else's mold.

Eventually, this started to take a toll on my wellbeing, often manifesting as burning pangs in my solar plexus. On the outside I had it all; on the inside I was twisted up like a pretzel and experienced an underlying feeling of sadness. I felt trapped.

Finally, it came to a point where I needed to make a decision: continue living someone else's life or choose to let go and *reclaim* my own. I chose the latter. This was not an easy process, in fact it was downright painful; yet, it was imperative if I was to realign myself with my true north. No more hiding in order to keep up with the Joneses, family, friends, colleagues, or society. And, to say NO to those around me who were projecting their own fears on to me by telling me I was running away. I wasn't running from something, you see, I was running toward something and that something was and is ME!

To live life according to ME. And to realize self-care is not selfish. That alone was a huge obstacle for me to overcome. I had always put others before myself and felt guilty when I did otherwise.

Until one day I woke up and realized I no longer had to prove anything to anyone. I only had to prove it to myself. The question then became, how do I create the new life I desired? I had no idea, but

I knew that I needed to make a change in order for change to occur. Since I was a child, I had always felt a pull to the West Coast—that it was a place where I would fully flourish. When considering the move, I initially came up with a laundry list of excuses that I thought were keeping me from moving forward. Then I realized, the only stop sign was fear. Fear of failure, judgment, and even love. It also occurred to me that my mom had been my only real anchor to the East Coast, but she had been gone for ten years at that point, so what was my real excuse? And in that moment of enlightenment, I could hear my mom whisper—"GO. Let go and GO!"

And, off I went! I packed up three suitcases and my little puggle, Lola and headed west. It certainly wasn't easy to pick up and move clear across the country. I owned a home in New Jersey, had huge clients based on the East Coast, and had never lived far from my lifelong friends and family. But I put several plans in place and told myself that I needed to trust the process and recalibrate as needed. It was in my power to make a choice and to *keep choosing* based on what I WANTED and what would fill my soul tank.

This move to the West Coast provided me the space and perspective shift I so desperately needed. I moved into a tiny studio in Santa Monica that overlooked the Pacific Ocean. At first it felt weird to say I rented when I had worked so hard to own my own place back east. But once I got past my ego, I realized how freeing it was not having the responsibilities of an owner, especially during this transformative process.

I also totally immersed myself in the outdoor lifestyle. Connecting with nature and breathing in that ocean air was definitely my church. I hiked or biked every day. I cut back on work commitments, started meditating and practicing yoga, and spent a lot of time with Lola at the beach. Watching her have a blast on the sand made my heart smile. Our walks back east had always coincided with conference calls or some other work-related tasks. Now, I was present with her, and with more things in my life.

I spent the next two years in Santa Monica, giving my soul exactly what it needed to heal. I let go of most of my East Coast-based clients and put my production company on hold to try on a staff position in LA. Though I had no clear plan, everything seemed to be magically falling into place (a new concept for me).

By year three, I was ready to plant two feet in the sand. I rented another place on the beach in Marina del Rey; it was open and airy with more incredible ocean views—Heaven on earth. And, it was here that I truly began my transformation.

Though I loved California, the year of being on staff had left me completely overworked and depleted. At forty years old, I realized I was done with the career I'd had for almost half my life. Did I stay with something for the money and familiarity, or pursue my life's greatest passion? I had finally figured out what my calling was— to serve others. Throughout my diverse career, I'd found that my greatest gifts and passion reside in my connections with people. I was always happiest and at my best when I was sharing my experiences and strategies to inspire and motivate my teams. But how did I start over, and from scratch?

I decided to parlay my business expertise and personal experiences into life and leadership coaching. For the next year I enrolled myself in various self-development classes and mindfulness programs. In 2015, I launched Change It Up, LLC. My biggest mission is to help others overcome fear and limiting beliefs so they too can live a life full of great abundance (on their terms).

Parallel to my huge career shift, I fell in love. That's the thing about changing our mindset and belief system—our energy shifts on all fronts, not just the one we happen to be focused on. Like attracts like, and I was emitting different vibes for sure! I had never really felt fulfilled in my romantic relationships, and no wonder. I never really had clarity or truth around my deepest needs and desires and fear always prevented me from living my authentic purpose.

Now, this would end up being the love of all loves. The one I now call my wife, Nicole. Yes! I ended up marrying a woman! I was with men my whole life but always felt there was something missing. However, I was always too scared to explore this until I decided to be true to myself, tap into my authentic heart, and live a "pang free" life.

It's approaching seven years since I boarded that plane to California. I'm beyond grateful to be living my abundant life with soulful purpose. Nicole and I recently bought a beautiful home in the sweetest beach town in San Diego, and I moved my business down here as well. This is truly the life I have craved since I was a child. I completely manifested this. And, yes, it certainly is BEAUTIFUL.

ABOUT THE AUTHOR: Nina Antinora is a life and leadership coach, mindfulness practitioner, and founder of Change It Up, LLC. She started her two-decade career in television, then transitioned into the corporate events arena—leading massive production, creative, and cross-functional strategic teams for global Fortune 500 companies. Nina now teaches the importance of mindfulness in the workplace, empathic leadership, and soft skills to improve communication, collaboration, and performance. With her personal clients, she offers one-on-one and group coaching, private retreats, and pioneered TrailChats,™ the first of its kind in SoCal. Nina is also developing e-courses to empower others to CHANGE IT UP & RECLAIM THEIR LIVES!

Nina Antinora
Change It Up, LLC.
changeitup.com
nina@changeitup.com
424-222-8088

Spiritual Authenticity
Trisha Schmalhofer

S pirituality is about connection. What began as a search outside myself ultimately led me inward to find it. To me, "it" is God. Divine Source, Infinite Spirit, Creative Life Force, and the Universe are all other names I have embraced during my life. God doesn't seem to mind me changing the name around. And through this connection to God, I am intertwined on a multidimensional web with everything else. On the microscale, this is my cells, organs, muscles. Going outward, it's my family, friends, all fellow Earth-lings, and Nature. Further outward are my ancestors, Spirit Guides, Angels, the galaxy. Once I really embraced this connection, inward and outward had no meaning and it became all the same. We are all connected and it is ALL God.

If I am being spiritually authentic then I connect to God in the way that works for me in that moment, in that phase of my life, whether other people understand or not. My spiritual practices are a combination of many different religions, belief systems, books of all subjects, classes, retreats, rituals, experiences, and guidance from human and Spirit teachers. I am a bit of a seeker and knowledge junkie who collects resources for "advice" and communicates with everything. I talk to trees…and Jesus…and books…and my body… and dolphins. Over the course of my journey, I have developed the gifts of hearing, seeing, feeling, and smelling Spirit. Sometimes I just simply know things. I don't push my practices on anyone, but am more than happy to share my experience or suggestions if they ask. Once I became connected to various aspects of God, the spiritual unfolding began; journeying through emotional, mental, and physical layers to remember who I am at the inner core, so I can fully emanate my soul gifts outward to others. Now I see mistakes and obstacles as learning opportunities to grow and deepen. Here are a few steps of my journey…

Twelve years of Catholic school was my spiritual foundation. The Catholic God is the Trinity—three in one: an all-knowing being in heaven, a man named Jesus who died for my sins, and the Holy Spirit who took the form of a dove and tongues of fire. God was not like me, but a mythological creature I couldn't seem to connect with. We were trained to say memorized prayers and do certain things at mass, but I didn't understand what it all meant. It wasn't until later in my adult life that I decided to go on a quest to discover MY Jesus. I voraciously read books, attended bible studies in every denomination, and went to classes and retreats. It turns out, my Jesus is a bad-ass I wanted to be like. He was a radical who brought about change and challenged the suppressors, a legendary healer who channeled the Holy Spirit through His hands, voice, and even His robe, a master of shamanism, quantum mechanics, and mediumship. He was a teacher who empowered His students to surpass what He did. He would go off alone all the time to pray, contemplate, and communicate with God. There were many times I called on Jesus when I was struggling emotionally and mentally. At first I would feel Him beside me, giving me love and support. Then, over time, I began to feel Him inside my heart guiding me and sending love through me.

In my college days, before my Jesus experiences, I had no spiritual practice and yet was becoming more sensitive to energy around me. I know now that this was some of my psychic abilities trying to develop, but back then I didn't have a clue. I was a decent student but started drinking, smoking pot, and overeating compulsively to ease these feelings. Many nights after partying I would end up an emotional wreck, crying and hating myself. In my twenties, I added hallucinogenics to alter reality and give me a false sense of a deeper connection to my surroundings. It took a toll on my body and my relationships and eventually I ended up in twelve-step recovery programs. I walked into my first meeting expecting to see society's outcasts. What I found was a connected community of people full of laughter who shared their struggles and solutions with honesty and authenticity. This framework of steps brought about a series of spiritual awakenings that allowed me to shift from feeling overwhelmed and disconnected to feeling free and expansive.

Once I decided to be honest, openminded, and willing, I partnered with a loving and caring God, was taught to go inward to identify and process emotions, take ownership of my mistakes, repair relationships with others and myself, and begin to learn how to trust myself and others.

My spiritual journey deepened when I became a massage therapist. I intuitively knew where to put my hands and how much pressure to apply to the muscles. This led me to a wonderful therapy called CranioSacral. With a gentle touch we can feel deep inside the body and work with an interconnective web of tissue throughout the body and a rhythmic pulse that emanates from the central nervous system. It is through these systems that we communicate with the person's Inner Physician. During a training class, an instructor led a visualization that took me to meet my own Inner Physician. This powerful connection opened up my world of self-empowerment and awareness that there is consciousness inside the cells and tissues of my body. With regular bodywork and visualizations, I began seeing my Inner Physician as my Higher Self—the Divine aspect of me that is directly connected to God and has access to universal wisdom.

Recently, in a shamanic studies class, I learned Higher Self places a piece of itself, a seed of light, in us at birth. This concept rang true to me. As this relationship with my Higher Self got stronger, my awareness of God, Spirit helpers and Angels increased, and my psychic gifts began getting clearer and more reliable.

Over the years, several people suggested I learn Reiki, which is a specific way of working with Life Force Energy, but I was turned off by Reiki Masters who seemed a bit egotistical. During a session with a client, I heard a Spirit Guide say in a taunting tone, "You know, this would be much easier if you knew Reiki…that's right, I said it…REIKI." I couldn't help but laugh out loud. My first Reiki attunement was powerful and broke me open (in a good way). During the attunement or activation, I could feel Jesus, "the Marys", and an assembly of other Masters, Angels, and Guides in the room ready to support and assist me. I could feel the warm, healing "God love" throughout my being. My second and third level attunements were just as expansive outwardly and deepening inwardly. My psychic gifts became even stronger and "aha" moments occurred several times a day. Spirit Teachers from across time began visiting me during therapy sessions to assist and teach me new concepts I haven't found in any books. I now teach Reiki to others to empower them to embrace their own Inner Physician and Higher Self, develop their psychic gifts, become aware of their team of helpers, and live their Soul Purpose.

My mother's illness and death was a profound piece of my journey. We were estranged for a while, and by the time we reunited her memory was already starting to diminish. Mom was diagnosed with dementia and had to be placed in a nursing home. I flew home often to continue healing our relationship and do CranioSacral and Reiki with her. During the sessions, Mom's Inner Physician led me to various parts of her brain, nervous system, and emotional centers. I wanted to ask her why she had this disease (because, to be honest, I didn't want to get it) but she could no longer speak.

One day, I was spiritually guided to connect with Mom's Higher Self and ask her. Though I had not been trained in this, I intuitively knew how to do it. I meditated and connected with my Higher Self, then asked to connect with Mom's. I could see her in Spirit form and asked why she had dementia. "Anger is eating my brain," she replied. Wow! This pushed me to get better at forgiving and releasing emotions. Mom passed surrounded by her family, and I had the privilege of seeing her Angel come for her and take her up a golden path. As incredible as this was, I felt sad and a bit lost that the woman who had brought me into this world was gone. But this was not the end of Mom's story. While viewing her body and placing flowers on her chest, I heard her voice say: *I can be a better mother to you now. I can see everything from here.* I cried so many different kinds of tears that day. Our relationship has continued to heal even after her physical death.

Nature has always been a source of healing and teaching for me. A walk through the park or in the mountains has always been a meditation. Oftentimes, I get answers to my questions from a bird or a horse or the ocean or whatever crosses my path. I am open and ready to receive the messages. It is through working with the natural world that I have come to really understand the web of connection. One of my first memories is toddling in my backyard with Tonya, our white German Shephard, walking beside me. She was my guardian and my friend who made me feel safe and loved. I recently had an experience with dolphins in the waters of the Bahamas. When these evolved, galactic beings healed me, I could hear and feel electrical currents running through my entire being. Their booming message to me was, *We are all one. Everything you need is inside you.* This provoked a huge shift in consciousness for me.

As I deepen and expand my connection to God/Higher Self and increase my awareness, I see that there is information and guidance all around me to assist on my life path. Since everything is connected, the message can come from any person, book, song, tv show, animal, cloud, or body of water. I shift my spiritual practice to complement or balance out what is happening in my life. Sometimes I need more meditation and rest; sometimes more dancing and exercise; and sometimes more social interaction and laughter. I regularly empty out my spiritual toolbox and take stock of what resources are in there. Oftentimes I add a new tool and occasionally take something out that doesn't serve me anymore. The history of my life and new experiences all add to the spiritual unfolding that makes me authentically me.

ABOUT THE AUTHOR: Trisha Schmalhofer is a Licensed Massage and CranioSacral Therapist, Certified Soul Realignment Practitioner, Scientist of the Spirit, Life Guide Mentor, Reiki Practitioner, teacher, health intuitive, retreat facilitator, and speaker. She blends medical modalities with ancient techniques, healing tools and traditions, and wisdom channeled from Divine Source to create a balanced approach tailored to meet each client's needs. Trisha leads numerous classes: Align! Be Your Authentic Self, Working with Your Inner Physician, Spiritual Development, Animal Communication and Healing, Quantum Planet Healing, and Medical Reiki. In her "Healing Party" program, held in homes or businesses, everyone receives Divine messages/guidance and connects with their Inner Healer.

Trisha Schmalhofer
MedHealers
MedHealers.com
MedHealersinfo@gmail.com
772-559-1993

Planting the Seeds of Authenticity

Paula D'Amico

We are all strongly connected to our parents….They raise us, guide us, teach us, dream for us, and above all LOVE us. This love creates a paternal bond that lasts a lifetime and beyond.

Back in 2005, my family life was blissful. My husband and I had careers we enjoyed, our handsome son was in first grade, we had a wonderful new group of friends, and our home was amazing. Mom and Dad lived only six blocks away, and my sister was about to come home and get married. We were living a simple, happy, and beautiful life.

Then the tsunami hit. A storm that would upend our world and irrevocably change our lives forever. It was also when my awakening began.

On New Year's Day, my father went into the hospital, never to return home.

Over the next few months, the bond between us grew ever stronger. We shared some deep conversations, but oftentimes they were very light and filled with stories of the grandson he adored. No matter what was ailing Dad that day, those stories never failed to light up his face with joy. Sometimes we prayed together; other times, words were not necessary at all. The silence between us wasn't just golden…it was *powerful*. His eyes, his voice, his touch as we held hands would be engrained in my memory forever.

A graduate of Cornell University of Horticulture, Dad had a

deep, lifelong love of nature. To make him feel more at home, we transformed his hospital room into a garden, filling it with plants and flowers on the walls and windowsills. We even created a garden on the bulletin board. And of course, there was music. We used music to calm all of our souls.

Just weeks before all this transpired, my husband was laid off. What had at first appeared to be devastating news turned out to be a true blessing. While I sat by my father's bedside, my husband spent hours of quality time with our son, forging a bond that might not have been possible if he was still working. In the midst of this painful time, it was a beautiful gift—one of many.

As Dad's journey to heaven approached, our small circle of hope became a strong circle of love, faith, and gratitude. Each day this circle continued to expand with more family, more friends, and some of the most amazing caregivers.

Fast forward a little more than two months to March 15, 2006... the Ides of March. The night was clean, clear, and crisp; the sky was breathtaking, the moon was full, and the earth was still. My father lay in his hospital bed surrounded by the nurses who had become our family, our angels. They helped prepare Dad for the next leg of an incredible journey...the next chapter in his life everlasting.

After hours of keeping watch, it was time to say farewell.

So, with music playing in the background, a candle glowing, and all of us by my father's side, we said our tearful goodbyes and watched him take his final breath.

And just like that...

It was done.

Like Christ on the cross.

My heart died.

I can still feel that moment, and it hurts. It physically hurts.

And at that moment, memories rushed through my head. It was like a scene from a movie...but this was no movie...this was OUR life.

Skating on our backyard ice rink and toasting marshmallows...

The swimming pool and the oasis my father created around it...
Swinging on a swing set...
The tent my father put up in our backyard...
Torches burning at night...
Planting marigolds...
Cutting bouquets of flowers to put in vases all over the house...
Watching moon flowers bloom as the summer sun set...
Picking green beans...
Dad standing at the grill...
Games...cookies...music...dancing...
Family gatherings that took all week to prepare for and culminated with a party that started early and went late into the night...
Years of Christmases...Easters...Thanksgivings... Halloweens... and birthday celebrations...

Even images of my father walking out from work, all grungy and ready to go home and dig into the garden and just be with his family.

This was a man who celebrated every season and made even the simplest of moments special.

When he left this world, it left a hole in my heart, a hole I never thought I could fill. How was I to move on? My father—the man who taught me how to love, have faith in God, be the best I can be, and be the best parent I can be—was now gone. Life fell silent.

After that, I cried a lot. I journaled. I even went to grief counseling. Nothing filled that hole. My husband was a great comforter but at some point, he didn't know what else to do. It was something my six-year old son said that finally woke me up. Looking at my husband, he whispered into his ear, "Why is Mommy so sad all the time?"

I knew I had to do something. But what?

As soon as I made this decision—and asked how to go about it—I got call from my best friend. She was on a mission to find natural remedies for her daughter who was dealing with some medical issues. She invited me to join her and learn about this "holistic" community she was discovering. Though I had never even heard the word holistic,

I accepted. Little did I know what doors were about to open for me; little did I know that I was about to take the first step on the road to healing and rediscovering my true self.

Have you ever walked into a place for the very first time and instead of feeling odd or out of place, you felt completely at home? Have you ever met a group of people who from the first hello felt like family? This is exactly how I felt with every first step into an expo, class, meeting, session, and appointment. But it was way beyond familiar, it was Divine Intervention, and it was healing me. I was reconnecting to a part of myself that I had not seen nor felt since I was a child.

Of all the holistic modalities I was interested in, the one I was drawn to most was Feng Shui. Actually, it was a combination of Feng Shui and a belief system that spans the globe and dates back to the beginning of time. It is the belief that nature has gifted us with all we need; that every plant, grain, mineral, and resin has meaning, and when you introduce them with purpose into your life, you help heal yourself physically and spiritually. Your world changes.

Whoa! That revelation jumpstarted my heart. I had always loved plants, loved gardening, and loved the sounds of nature, so embracing their power was the perfect fit. Like a hungry teenager, I devoured everything I could get my hands on—books, articles, and classes. I started incorporating more plants—living and dried—into my life, my home, and of course my garden.

Remember the comfort and familiarity I felt when I started this healing journey? Well, it was now ten times stronger! Why? Because as a speaker and horticulturalist, that's what my dad did. It was that undeniable connection between us, a connection that not even his death could sever.

And my amazing and beautiful mother? She was a true teacher in every sense of the word. Beautiful from the inside out. People, no matter their age, gravitated toward her presence. She was oozing with love, positive energy, creativity, and spirituality.

And to watch Mom and Dad together was pure magic. Theirs was a true partnership that could only have been Divinely created. What made my parents so incredible was the power of their simplicity. They were humble, loving, faithful people who were 110% AUTHENTIC, and they led by example.

This is the seed they planted within me. This is the plant I nurture. This is the harvest I reap, not just for me but for others.

Years after discovering how healing the power of nature is for me (and with a little push from my family and friends) I took a leap of faith, starting a business that utilizes the healing gifts my parents have given me: teaching, speaking, and planting.

TEACHING: Revealing ancient traditions using the power of nature.

SPEAKING: Sharing my plant passion so others can embark on their own healing journey.

PLANTING: Allowing others to re-connect with the beauty and power that surrounds them.

Think back to when you were a child. Do you remember how amazing the world was around you?

The brilliant colors and shapes of every petal on every flower...

The tender feel of blades of grass under your feet...

The healing touch of water...

The fresh scent of lilacs and lilies...

These are the gifts we all have been given. Over the years we may have forgotten how something that doesn't cost a dime can help balance and connect us with our authentic self. This something is time. How long has it been since you took time for yourself?

If we just take a moment, we will remember who we are inside. There is such beauty and power in taking a break. Why? Because it's your time. No one can infringe upon what makes you feel content, happy, or rejuvenated. For me, balance comes in many forms.

Closing my eyes and listening to the sound of rain on a warm summer day...

A gentle breeze caressing my face...

The sound of leaves mimicking the sound of rain...
The smell of dried leaves in the Fall...
The crackling sound of a campfire...
Placing my hands in the dirt....
Creating an orchestra of healing color and scents as I garden.

It is amazing what happens when we take a moment to step away from our hurried lives, put our face in the sun, and just breathe. Even on a cold winter's day, all it takes is one good burst of warm sun and we are re-energized.

At one time, I felt so empty; blind to the beauty of the world around me. Every time I sat in silence, I would only feel sorrow.

Today, my life is no longer silent, but filled with incredible sounds, smells, and signs of new life. I even recognize the power of my own breath, and I know the moment I connect to this power is the moment I find my true, authentic self. The same is true for you. Why? Because it is your body and only you can experience that amazing power within.

I teach, plant, love, pray, and share the knowledge my parents have passed down to me with others. With every word I type, with every message that flows from my lips, every tender plant nestled in the soil and combination of flowers created, with every home blessed, I feel Mom and Dad in my heart. Their energy flows through me and out into those who need it, delivering healing to all. It is a pure gift that keeps on giving to any and all who wish to receive it.

We are all on a journey.

We are searching for answers, love, hope, light, and comfort.

We are trying to find our purpose as we travel through this physical life.

Allowing nature to take its course has opened my heart and soul to so many amazing people, places, and experiences. It has helped me to heal from heartache, find my strength, dig deep to uncover my authentic self, and share it with others.

In the beginning I was afraid; then I learned how to trust.

I put my faith in what I cannot see, and I followed my heart.

The rest just followed—or should I say—flowed.

It's not easy to do, but once you discover what your passions are, they begin to bloom—one flower after another—until you have a garden. It is the garden of your life. All you need to do is tend to it and share the beauty, and the rest will take care of itself.

ABOUT THE AUTHOR: Paula is a wife, mother, television producer, speaker, teacher, and founder of Blessings by Nature®, a company with a mission to deliver hope and healing into people's lives using the power of plants. Paula's love of nature dates back to her childhood, when she worked side by side in the dirt with her horticulturist father. Over the past decade, Paula has studied how the simple placement of plants, along with the use of Feng Shui, can transform one's life. She shares her passion for plants through a variety of inspiring hands-on lectures and workshops. Paula also serves as president of the Holistic Chamber of Commerce - Downtown Buffalo Chapter.

Paula D'Amico
Blessings by Nature
blessingsbynature.com
info@blessingsbynature.com
716-348-4125

Re-Membering Eden:
Community's Hidden Treasures
Kathy Sipple

If we identify the conditions that allow groups to thrive and flourish, we can consciously design them into our group structures. We can seed our groups in healthy soil, and create movements that are truly inclusive and welcoming to all of us, in the full complexity of who we are. And when we do, all of our important work becomes more effective. ~ Starhawk

A Taste of Heaven

I am born in 1966, to a loving family with devoted parents and two sisters. I grow up in Audubon Park, an enchanting urban jewel in the midst of Louisville, Kentucky known for its majestic trees, friendly neighbors, and beautiful older homes. I delight in climbing my favorite tree in the far corner of our yard. From my perch, I sometimes converse with my patient, octogenarian neighbor, Ms. Lila.

"How come you have flowers growing next to your tomatoes?" I ask.

"They're very good friends!" she tells me. "They help each other out to make food and keep pests away."

I am happy, safe, and supported. I have everything I need in my familiar, close-knit little world.

Transplanted

One key concept to successful transplanting is when a plant has "hardened off." Plants growing outside naturally acclimate to changing weather. These plants have toughened up

for the winter, but plants grown in an environmentally-controlled greenhouse must be prepared before being transplanted.
~ *Nursery Management Magazine*

When I am eleven, my father gets a promotion that requires our family to relocate to Virginia. I begin at a new school in the fall. I miss my yard and my special tree. Initially I am shy and find it hard to make new friends. I yearn to be back "home." I keep in touch with my old friends through writing letters and occasional long-distance phone calls.

Eventually, I make new friends; however, it's soon time to move again, this time to Michigan. I notice changes in my accent—I pick up bits of the local dialect while retaining some of the former. I am becoming a hybrid. I'm not exactly "from" anyplace anymore and yet I now feel at home in several places. I begin to see being transplanted as a gift. If I had stayed in one place, I would not have gained this perspective; nor would I have developed empathy for others who find themselves on new soil.

Knowing what it feels like to be new awakens in me the desire to make others feel welcome and at home. I seek people out on the edges—the wallflowers—and engage them in conversation. My outreach leads me to volunteer at a senior center, visit a group home for adults with developmental disabilities, babysit for a child with autism...I want to know more about people who are different from me.

When it is time to head to college, I choose the University of Michigan in Ann Arbor, drawn by its cultural diversity and many trees as much as for its highly rated academics. I make many friends at college, from all walks of life.

Like most Economics majors, I study Money and Banking and Econometrics, along with micro- and macro-economic theory. I also take many nontraditional courses, including population growth, corporate environmental impact, sustainable forestry and fishing. I become a volunteer income tax assistant and am astounded at how little some people are surviving on. How is this economy I'm learning about working for them?

After graduation many of my classmates continue to graduate school to pursue MBAs or jobs on Wall Street. They see my beautifully prepared resume and ask for my help creating theirs, using newly emerging technology called desktop publishing. I don't have any special training in it, but I am good with writing and editing and am a quick learner. I get a job with a company that conducts desktop publishing workshops all over the country. I glean enough on-the-job training to land a job at a publishing firm doing page layout. My career progresses in a series of unpredictable stepping stones that take advantage of newly emerging opportunities as they present themselves. I trust my intuition that my path is leading me where I need to go.

My economics background continues to inform how I see the world and stokes my curiosity about money. Despite my unconventional career path, I manage to buy a home on my own before I am thirty. I save for retirement. I am playing by society's rules, but I am tired of them. I read *Your Money or Your Life: 9 Steps to Transforming Your Relationship with Money and Achieving Financial Independence*. It strikes a chord—the book calls into question assumptions about why we must dress in power suits and drive cars to impress our clients. Who are we buying these for? What are the costs to maintain a life of appearances rather than the one we actually want to live? It was a question I had never allowed myself to ask. I begin to think about what I really want and what I want is love, to be someone's partner in life and to do work that doesn't feel so much like work.

Companion Planting

Life without love is like a tree without blossoms or fruit.
~ Khalil Gibran

Soon after I open to the possibility of true love, I meet John. We date long-distance for several years before I sell my house and move to Chicago to be with him. It feels scary to give up all I have built, but missing out on love and a chance to become more fully who I am is scarier.

Living in Chicago provides access to many new spiritual learning opportunities. I study A Course in Miracles, Kabbalah, Akashic Records, HeartMath, Reiki, and Yoga. One day right after yoga class, I head to the grocery store to pick up some items for dinner and right there in the checkout line, a feeling of overwhelming love rushes over me. I suddenly see strangers differently—they are all so beautiful, and illuminated! I know I am becoming a different person, more fully capable of loving John, the world—and myself too.

I have been in Chicago about a year when the attacks of September 11th happen. Suddenly the city feels constrictive and John and I both yearn to be somewhere "away" and peaceful, at least for the night. When we cross the border into Indiana I see a coyote in the highway median; something tells me if I am where this creature is living, I am safe.

A desire to settle down and for more connection with nature leads us to move to Valparaiso, Indiana. It's within an hour's drive of the Chicago Loop but feels a world away. I am thirty-six when we marry and my biological clock is beginning to tick more loudly. After much soulful consideration John and I determine parenting is not our path and yet I still long to birth something that is bigger than me, bigger than us.

Vale of Paradise

The only downside to living in Valparaiso is the scarcity of jobs. I become an online marketing consultant and trainer since using the internet, I can work anywhere. As social media marketing emerges I find I am fascinated to integrate it into my offerings. I realize how extensive my own social network has become since I reached out to friends and family from past places I worked and lived. It allows us to share information and resources that make us feel connected and up to date with important life happenings beyond a yearly Christmas card or occasional email or call.

When I am not working, I often explore one of the many nearby nature preserves or parks. Through my hikes in the woods, I become fascinated with the diverse flora and fauna. I take a special interest in mushrooms. I take courses through the Hoosier Mushroom Society to learn more. I learn that what most people refer to as a mushroom is only the visible fruiting body; fungi are made up of tiny threads called mycelium. These form extensive underground networks, connecting the roots of different plants in an area, even different species, together, allowing them to communicate. Mycologist Paul Stamets, calls this network "the internet of the forest."

I learn about a scientist in British Columbia named Suzanne Simard, who is researching tree communication and networking. "Mother trees", the biggest, oldest trees in the forest with the most fungal connections, are not necessarily female, but Simard sees them in a nurturing, supportive, maternal role. With their deep roots, they draw up water and make it available to shallow-rooted seedlings. They help neighboring trees by sending them nutrients, and when the neighbors are struggling, mother trees detect their distress signals and increase the flow of nutrients accordingly.

That's it, I decide. I may not become a biological mother, but I will become a Mother Tree in my community! I will find a way to harness the power of the internet to tap our hidden networks and assets to help my community recognize its abundance. I am inspired to think about the people I encounter who don't fit into the traditional economy, meaning they do not have a place to go to get their needs fulfilled or to share their own gifts.

Research leads me to timebanking. A timebank is a service exchange where members exchange services using time-based social currency rather than money. Everyone's time is valued equally. Unlike bartering, members can bank time and spend it with any other member in the timebank, not just the member they earned time credit from. An important timebank concept is reciprocity—it acknowledges that everyone has gifts to share and must do so to feel valued.

When a part-time coordinator position becomes available for ValpoNEXT, a new nonprofit with a vision of making Valparaiso the most civically engaged city of our size, I apply right away and get the job. I take every opportunity I can find to learn how to do my job better. I attend a two-day workshop on Asset Based Community Development (ABCD). I take a course on Civic Reflection. I become a facilitator for the Pachamama Alliance and take their Game Changer Intensive course. I have the impulse to share what I know with a wider audience so more communities can benefit.

Flower of Life

In early 2019 I join the Evolutionary Ambassadors Academy with Barbara Marx Hubbard. Barbara has been a hero of mine since I read her book, *Conscious Evolution*, many years ago.

Barbara developed a process called synergistic convergence (SynCon for short). The method involves participants entering the Wheel of Co-Creation which is divided into sectors such as Health, Education, Governance, Media, etc. We are to participate in the first ever online SynCon and I am excited to help with the technology and planning to ensure its success. One of the ambassadors described the SynCon experience as big as the lunar landing! We continue to meet and refine the process.

After the first SynCon, I continue to dream vivid dreams about the Flower of Life, a pattern in sacred geometry that has always interested me. I see the pattern superimposed over the Wheel of Co-Creation, allowing a relationship network map to be created among the initial ambassadors and rippling out in waves as each of us invite our own networks and others join in the evolutionary process.

I see the world, connected by strands of light and love, the thinking layer of Earth, the noosphere. Discovering our talents, having a community to share them with and finding the resources needed is all within our reach. When we do this, we will have re-membered each of us to our rightful place in the Garden of Paradise. We will have restored Eden in our time.

ABOUT THE AUTHOR: Kathy Sipple resides just outside of Chicago near the Indiana Dunes with her husband John and their black Labrador retriever, Bodhi. She is a frequent keynote speaker and trainer and host of 219 GreenConnect podcast. She holds a B.A. in Economics from the University of Michigan and is a member of Mensa. She won a Golden Innovator Award from Barbara Marx Hubbard and Conscious Evolutionaries Chicagoland for her empowering and groundbreaking work in social media. Sipple works online with clients everywhere to provide social media strategy, training, and coaching.

Kathy Sipple
Consciously Connecting Community
kathysipple.com
kasipple@gmail.com
219-405-9482

Coming Home on the Grand Canyon Trail

Nancy Stevens

Until recently, I defined the scope of my life as average and ordinary. Overcoming things like abuse, neglect, addiction, or any major setback weren't part of my life's fabric. Instead, I spent years posturing so I would fit in with the status quo. Along the way a collection of emotional baggage—good, bad, and ugly—set up shop in my psyche. My unspoken "job" was to accept without question my emotions and feelings while allowing others to set the tone for who I was and how I lived. I gave myself permission to live life as I thought it should be—at surface level.

For reasons unknown to me, I was afraid to plunge the depths of who I was and sit with my baggage. I guess I was afraid of finding out—and revealing to everyone else—that my life was really a lackluster waste. It never dawned on me that I actually could do more, that I didn't need to wait for someone or something outside of me to make it happen. For years I locked the door on anything change-related; I didn't understand that even when we brace ourselves against change, it will flow in and through us as it needs to do to ensure the continuum of life.

It would be two completely unexpected encounters—or as I called them, change agents—that set the stage for the emotional transformation that allowed me to finally start showing up as myself. The first of these events took place at a yoga class when I was forty-one; the second was a few years later, during an extremely emotional energy healing session.

What emerged following these experiences was the realization that I had two distinct choices: stay comfortable and small within the confines of vicarious living, or dive in completely, carrying all fears, insecurities, joys, and wins to be dismantled and remodeled. The Universe/God was gently giving me a taste of what *could be*, but wouldn't, unless and until I took some bold steps forward.

Life Staging

When I look back on my childhood, I realize that I was not encouraged to question any deep emotions, especially the unpleasant ones. This was not due to any past trauma or abuse in my parents' lives, as they were both raised in loving homes; they simply had their own rules of how to be. I wasn't asked to share how I was truly feeling or why I might have acted out. Deeper feelings were private. Unspoken. My parents rarely cried, and when they did it was uncomfortable. My unconscious takeaway was this: crying was an embarrassing, even shameful, display of emotion. I began to equate vulnerability with weakness.

There were also many positive aspects to my upbringing. My parents were hardworking, loving, and kind. The credos they lived by were: Live honestly. Be loyal and kind. Work hard to have a comfortable good life. I was raised above all else to respect, honor, and submit to adult authority. I learned that *who I was* came from doing what was asked without resisting.

This included going along with painful teasing, about both my physical appearance and my last name, Ottenfeld, that occurred from my earliest school days through high school. Though the jokes hurt my feelings, I good-naturedly laughed at them; I even joked about myself to "one up" everyone else. I figured it was my way of fitting in, even if I was looking in from the outside.

Bigger Picture

I unconsciously gave power to these slights and derisive laughter because I felt I didn't belong, measure up or fit in. Fear quietly settled in my psyche, where it would establish residency for years. I began to live life from the passenger seat, waiting for the driver to show up and take me to the next destination.

Fast Forward - Adulting

As a married woman and mom to four sons I was so caught up with the day-to-day that I had no time (and no desire) for deeper thoughts of any kind. I placed my identity and who I was on what I externally did: wife, mom, small business owner, and volunteer. It was during this extremely busy season of living life as I thought it *should be* that things took a sudden turn, and took me to a level I had never sought out or anticipated.

It began with a heart-wrenching fall-out with a very close friend. She, along with her husband and children, were like family to us and losing them shook my entire world. I settled into a raw, wounded place of grief and victim mentality, and there I would remain, isolated and alone, for two full years, even as I continued to actively manage our sons, home, and business.

After years of suppressing and hiding from them, I had suddenly landed face to face with my untapped, raw emotions. It felt awful! I wish I had known at the time that I was actually experiencing a powerful awakening, that life was extending a hand so I could finally dive beneath the surface, process pain, and even embrace it as a tool for personal growth. This is what it means to be alive and involved. Life is beautifully messy; though of course at the time I didn't think it was beautiful at all.

On many levels, the loss of this friendship actually turned out to be preparation for other major life changes. My husband received an opportunity to be a songwriter and music producer in Nashville, and I suddenly found myself packing up our family for a cross-country move. Without our network to rely on, we now had to choose how we would craft our new life.

I wouldn't have thought it possible, but after settling in Nashville

I had even less time for myself. There was a local gym, however, that offered yoga classes during my limited window of freedom and I signed up.

During a space of silence and stillness at the end of class we were invited to lay on our mats and simply be—to rest and renew. This invitation, along with my teacher's loving touch and presence, gave birth to a tear-filled awakening. Suddenly I realized I was the one who mattered; I was enough. I had found my home—a place to tend to my heart, feelings, and needs.

This deep shift led to more classes and eventually, yoga teacher training. My studies included The Yoga Sutras, which helped me to learn the practice and philosophy of yoga more intimately. Of these, the one that stood out for me most was the philosophy of the Sutra "Ishvara Pranidhana." IP is the spiritual act of surrendering the self to the Divine while studying (being a student of faith or practice and belonging to one's faith) and trusting the wisdom of the Divine to guide the life and actions of the self in order to work in the world.

What spoke to me as I reflected and studied was the need for me—a Christian—to take up for my faith by reading The Holy Bible. I learned and more deeply embraced the tenets of my faith while inviting these elements into myself as a yoga student, teacher, wife, mom, and friend. It was through this practice that for the first time I began to show up in my life.

Through yoga I also began the practice of learning how to be present and mindful. Initially, this was quite a challenge, as it directly countered how I'd always lived, namely, in a state of reacting along with worst-case-scenario thinking. As time passed, I gradually incorporated mindfulness into every aspect of my life. It now showed up in how I processed my thoughts, feelings, and sticky life triggers while developing and using all of my senses. Learning how to live more mindfully cultivated a fertile soil that enriched my authentic self and gave it room to flourish.

I began to understand that life was not just a string of random happenings but a complex fabric of emotional application, self-regulation, compassionate reasoning, and releasing taking place each and every day.

I found one of the things I loved most about taking and teaching yoga classes was helping and offering life advice to other students. This led me to pursue a new place to "practice" yoga by becoming certified and credentialed as a health and life coach. Even as these new opportunities surfaced, however, I still held on to a strong untapped emotion—fear. I didn't know why I struggled when coaching was so fulfilling to me, though I did realize it was holding me back. Fear told me I wasn't meant to partner with others as their coach. I didn't know enough, wasn't good enough, and would never measure up to all the other successful healers and coaches who had "made it."

I did as fear told me to do—absolutely nothing. Self-loathing, victim thinking, and blaming settled in and took over what could have been.

Authenticity Encounter #2

Initially, when a good friend suggested I visit an energy healer, it didn't feel good to me. Not only did it go against my faith, it seemed like a desperate move. Luckily for me, God is not limited to human understanding but brings in who is needed, when they are needed. That's what I believe happened when, despite my misgivings, I decided to call and schedule an appointment.

There I was, waiting in the healer's office with no idea what to expect. The room was ordinary enough, with two chairs and a table with a box of tissues beside it. I vividly remember her asking me, oh so kindly, "What brings you here to see me today?" at which I burst forth in a river of tears. A box of tissues later, she began her work by asking me to be still and silent.

At one point I literally felt my entire body shift off the floor and land softly back. As our session came to a close I felt a soft warmth like a blanket fresh from the dryer literally cover me while a soft light illuminated her entire office. Although I can't quite put into words what happened, I left her office that day opened, cleansed, and changed internally. I had crossed over from living a fear-centered existence to trusting my intuition.

It was from this place I grew into an authentic, heart-centered woman. I learned how to walk into every part of my life—sometimes amazing, sometimes messy, sometimes sad—all of this the sum total of who I am today.

The Grand Canyon: Coming Full Circle

In 2012, we took a road trip from Nashville to Oregon. We decided to stop off at the Grand Canyon along the way, excited to see this natural wonder. Looking down from our touristy view I recall telling my husband my dream of someday hiking the uneven twists to the bottom floor. This hike would be a benchmark in my process of embracing my body, mind, and spirit. While on this epic hike I would be set free!

Five years later, that dream became reality. My husband and I returned to the Grand Canyon and along with a trail guide descended the South Kaibab Trail to the bottom floor. After celebrating our journey by dipping our achy feet in the mighty, cold Colorado River, we set up camp at the Bright Angel Campsite. We spent two glorious nights beneath the stars before hiking back up on the Bright Angel Trail.

As I had imagined, the hike was powerfully symbolic of my journey of self-discovery and authenticity. This journey, with its many twists and turns, has been a complex and challenging process, a combination of practice, self-compassion and mindfulness that continues to this day. At times I'm comfortable, navigating each day with ease, and at other times I'm struggling with what is at hand. Such is the nature of being human. The difference is that now I live fully in all areas of my life; I embrace every aspect of how I came to be. I know who I am.

ABOUT THE AUTHOR: Nancy Stevens is an International Certified

Coach; blogger with The Wellness Universe; and a talk show host on "News For The Soul Radio.com," where she shares her passion and tips for cultivating authentic self-care. She is also an accomplished speaker, educating groups and organizations about personal development and healthy wellbeing. Nancy's calling is to connect and empower busy women to find and own their authentic identity so that they can be change-makers and positively impact others. When she's not working, Nancy loves spending time with her husband, a four-time Grammy Award winner, and their four sons.

Nancy Stevens
Nancy Stevens Coaching
nancystevenscoaching.com
nancy@nancystevenscoaching.com
615-887-8208

The Sound of Authenticity
Andrea Austin

"**A**re you happy?"

This innocent question, asked as I was leaving a yoga class by my teacher/friend, felt like a hard slap to my face. It was May 2009, and I was about to leave for the Turks and Caicos Islands, my ideal vacation spot and the one place I thought would make me happy.

But that question jolted me so significantly that, for the first time ever, I actually thought about it. *Was* I happy? I began to really look at my life and it suddenly seemed as if I had been living in a fog, walking through the motions but going nowhere. I was forty-two and had a great husband, two kids, and a dog; I also had the house, the cottage, a fifty-thousand-dollar boat, and a six-figure job as a CA/CPA for a large international accounting firm. What more could a girl ask for? Yet, there I was, so exhausted I couldn't get out of bed before ten a.m. Nothing was new; it was as if I was repeating the same patterns over and over again.

I thought of that question, even as I lay in my condo on the beach, breathing the fresh sea air through the open window. One day during that trip I was standing in the kitchen when suddenly I felt myself leave my body. As I hovered in the air, I heard my soul yell at me, "Are you happy?" and could no longer deny the answer. It was a resounding *no*. I was at the pinnacle of my career and had other wonderful people in my life, yet I was miserable and in a lot of pain.

That pain had started at the age of eighteen, when I came down with a mysterious illness that no one seemed able to understand or help with. Over the next several decades I did everything I could to get help with the extreme digestive issues, headaches, and backaches. I went to a chiropractor, had sinus surgery, and tried physiotherapy, Reiki, myofascial release work, tai-chi, massage, and energy work. I even saw a psychologist for eight years after the birth of my first son to help me stay strong and keep my shit together 'cause, dammit, I had a life to live and I was going to live it. But most days it felt like pushing through mud. Pushing myself to perform, to be a great mom, a great friend and family member, and a great employee, and losing it every now and then, only to pick up the pieces and move forward. In all of this pushing, however, I was losing me. The real me that wanted to play, be real, and do life differently, but didn't know how. I was stuck in my reality and could not get out. And let's be real, I wasn't willing to wait to retirement to make all that happen.

That out-of-body experience in Turks and Caicos was the turning point. It led to my saying yes to another getaway—this time a girls' weekend in Nova Scotia where I drew my first set of angel cards. They told me everything I needed to know, if I was willing to listen. You see, I have come to realize that the key to happiness is to listen to the messages I am given and then be willing to say yes when the Universe presents me with an opportunity for change. We are designed for growth and I had been stagnant for far too long. It was time to step out of the box.

That weekend led to my decision to take a one-year sabbatical from my job. Going from six figures to zero was a BIG leap, especially since I had been working to support myself since I was fourteen. But somehow I knew if I didn't change something, I wasn't going to make it. I realized I had been lying to myself, over and over, trying to convince myself that I was happy. That one moment of clarity allowed me to see the lie. It also made me ask the question, "What if there is another way? Another path to follow that was authentically me and it took me to places, people, and a life I could not imagine?" That's exactly what happened to me during my time off.

In 2012 I remember sitting at my aunt's funeral, watching and observing the many beautiful people who showed up to show their love and support. My aunt was a beautiful, loving being who appeared to have it all; yet beneath her seemingly perfect life, she, like the rest of my family, struggled to be "okay" in this world, to be loved, and not live life from fear and insecurity. *Why does that happen?* I asked myself, and in that moment I decided that I was going to do things differently; I was not going to repeat those patterns in my life.

The Universe heard me. Four weeks later, while attending the Toronto Yoga Show, I was introduced to a technology—and to a person—that would change my destiny forever. That technology was a sound-based instrument designed to shift consciousness (not that I knew what that word even meant!); the person was Bill, my divine partner. Though I didn't understand any of my choices, those days I was doing things that felt right to my soul, even if it meant saying yes to a show I used to make fun of! The same was true for Bill, who had decided to drive the 1700 miles from Regina to Toronto to attend the show, not because it was logical, but because it felt right.

I returned home from the show with my first set of "personal frequencies"—meaning they were based on the uniqueness of my voice—and began listening. Immediately, I noticed changes. I was relaxing, exploring, and more excited about my life than I had been in a long time. Most would attribute my new attitude to meeting Bill, but I knew inside that there was more going on. It felt like I had found a destiny. Turns out, both were true; in Bill I had found a partner in life, love, and business, and with whom I began an evolutionary journey. I had also committed to sharing a unique, consciousness-based technology that forever opened me up to finding and collaborating with other heart-centered beings who wanted to make a difference on this planet.

After years of illness, my body began to heal, just by using sound and scalar energy! These simple, crazy little sounds began to help me unravel and dissipate the emotional baggage that I had been carrying for most of my life. Now, without them weighing me down, I was free to uncover my real self, and how she wanted to live. I am not saying that this was a "magic pill." Along the way I had to make some choices that, while very tough, were for right for me, driven by my heart and soul, rather than my head. But these tools, along with amazing people and experiences along the way, taught me how to live differently; live a life of love and service, and arrive at a place where I had always wanted to be but could never reach.

Not everyone in my life was open to the changes I was making. One day shortly after my "Awakening," I was sitting in the car with my stepmother, trying to explain to her what I saw, what I felt, and what I knew was possible in this world; how humanity could actually choose to live and see life differently. She looked at me like I'd lost my ever-loving mind.

"What you're describing…" she said, "…people will have to want change."

I laughed when she said that, because I realized the truth of this, and that I wanted change; I was up for the ride. And what a ride it was. As I transitioned from my old life to the new, my family put up a fuss, a really big fuss. One night about five years after I'd met Bill, they finally had the courage to ask if I was "anti-establishment." I almost peed my pants! Imagine me, the ex-tax CA who worked with a large, reputable accounting firm and taught taxation at the University of Toronto for a number of years, anti-establishment? The funny thing is, if you asked me ten years earlier what I thought of the new me, I would have said the same thing. What my heart had led me to do was so radical to my family; they simply could not fathom it. Just because we follow our heart does not mean everyone is going to like it. Trust me, most don't. But as the bumper sticker my mother used to have on her car stated, "Why be normal?"

Normal is overrated.

When I think about my journey, I realize that it's been about helping to build awareness of other possibilities in life, love, and business, and how technology can help shift consciousness in the simplest of ways to help us <u>all</u> be more authentic, more beautiful, and stronger. It can help us let go of our shit. It may feel strange or uncomfortable at times, but that's just because it's new and unfamiliar. Imagine a hundred years ago if someone told you, "Hey, one day we're going to be able to talk to someone across the globe while sitting in a coffee shop with a phone that fits into our pants pocket"? You would have thought they were high, crazy or both. But that's what way-showers do—they bring into awareness things that most don't see as possible; they also help us get out of our heads and into our hearts to facilitate change. I never expected to be a way-shower, but nothing else has ever felt so right.

One day, while driving along, I found myself contemplating this chapter for the book and how I would finish it off. Driving has always almost been meditative for me—it is often when I get the most clarity. That day, I found myself looking back over the past seven years since that monumental day on April 1, 2012, and suddenly I saw all the patterns I have let go of, and at an accelerated rate, after decades of holding so tightly to them, in fear that I would lose control. And I started to cry, so filled was I with this deep recognition that my whole life had felt like a struggle to move forward, only to fall backwards. It was if I was being held by something I did not understand. All the therapies, discussions, help, and connections could not break me free from it. It was like I was Goliath, tethered by the strings of consciousness, stories, beliefs, and patterns all around me. I also felt like I did not "fit in," that I was playing a role because I was not sure what else to do. I kept feeling like I needed to live up to other people's and society's standards and expectations in order to fill a hole inside myself, just to feel good about myself.

Those tears as I stepped forward to complete this chapter were tears of joy for the authentic life I live today. I now see that life cannot be planned from the head, as I tried to do for my first forty-plus years on earth; it must flow from a willingness to listen to the heart. Most of life my heart was so scared and so shut down I had forgotten how to use her. Sometimes I think my dis-ease was really my body yelling, "Wake up and listen to your heart, sister, 'cause this ain't working for you!"

What is your heart telling you? Take some time to listen to your inner guidance, notice the fears that exist inside of you. Come join the ride of following life from the heart, not the mind, and explore tools that can help you let go of the fears that are stopping you from love.

ABOUT THE AUTHOR: Andrea Austin is the co-owner and founder of Clearly Conscious Energetics, a worldwide organization helping shift consciousness through the use of unique technologies that assist people in shifting limiting beliefs and fears that are holding them back from love. Andrea's career began as a CPA with an international accounting firm. After years of living with fear and insecurity, Andrea now shares what it's like to change from the inside out when you are willing to step into love, wake up and participate in life in an authentic way. Andrea is currently working on her book, "Journey into Love," due out in the fall of 2019.

Andrea Austin
Clearly Conscious Energetics
clearlyconscious.ca
ann@clearlyconscious.ca
647-294-8824

Rejection & Betrayal to Acceptance & Truth

Anna Trillana

"In order to write about life you first must live It." ~ *Hemingway*

We live in a culture where we are groomed to deny our essence as humans by shutting down our feelings and replacing them with immediate gratifications. We are driven to live by unattainable standards, to essentially be high-performing robots. We don't receive instruction manuals on how to do this. Instead, we are taught myths: "Don't feel bad," "Be strong," "Keep busy," "Replace the loss/stress," and "Time heals all." If we don't measure up, we are considered "not enough."

This, of course, is bullshit. How can anyone be stress-free when we are expected to behave like robots rather than humans? The truth is, humans are *complicated,* all perfectly imperfect (though, I prefer to say "we are all understandably perfectly f*cked!"). Thus, learning how to un-f*ck our imprinted, unhealthy habits is imperative if we are ever to achieve peace.

Compassion is gained by understanding that "we are all doing the best we can." Our wounds continue to reopen and bleed because we never had the proper aids to heal or address them. Traumas tempt us to travel down a steep dark slope to escape the pain, some never to return. My hope is for everyone to become aware that we have the potential to survive anything. Acceptance is gained when the truth sets you free. Accurate information is truth and light, which exposes these shadows, illusions, mirrors, and lies. Thus, awareness is one of the keys to healing. How can you change a light bulb if you can't see that it's burnt out? To truly heal is to acknowledge we are allowed to feel.

"I am not my past, I am who I choose to become." ~ Carl Jung

It has never been difficult for me to tell clients and friends about the challenges I've endured; I use it to teach, relate, and connect to others, to let them know they are not alone. However, I realized that I did resist *writing* my truth. It seemed every time I tried I would hear the voices of my family ringing in my head: "Your existence has brought us misery"; "I wish you were aborted"; "You will never amount to anything"; and "Don't tell anyone our family's history." Rejection, Neglect, Abuse, Betrayal, and Secrecy had become the themes of my life.

The lesson was loud and clear. When trying to heal our pains and wounds, we are often taught that we must rid ourselves of the ego; however, this is impossible, as it is part of our consciousness. Instead, we must utilize the ego. We must do conscious mental work. I realized that my physical and emotional triggers were giving me feedback I could use to realign myself, refocus my perception, and ultimately change my unhealthy coping mechanisms. No one was reopening my wounds; they didn't even know what they were. I was the one who was hurting myself by denying who I was.

I grew up with my aunt and grandmother, an arrangement I thought was normal because I didn't have anything to compare it to. Only later did I see the situation for what it was. There's a twelve-year age gap between me and my sister and two brothers. My parents stated they were too busy to care for me and created a weekends-only arrangement. Enter Neglect and Abandonment.

I also thought my abilities (which had begun in early childhood and never left me), to see spirits, feel others' feelings, hear others' thoughts, know things about their lives, and recall my past lives and newborn memories were normal. I didn't understand what others meant when I "heard" them call me a freak. Why was me helping others prevent them from getting into an accident "interfering"? Why did Grandfather visit me while they were at his funeral? Why was it acceptable for my grandma or elders to have "gifts" but I was deemed "cursed"? Why did my mother and father have such contempt in their eyes when they looked at me? Why wasn't I invited to family events, dinners, trips, or pictures? Why couldn't I get piano lessons, go to Sunday school, and take art classes, when they all did? Why were my birthdays never celebrated occasions, but ones in which fights took place? Enter Rejection.

From ages four to nine, I did learn a "game" that one of my siblings played with me, a game I thought was normal because the neighbour downstairs played it with me as well. When I told my grandma about this game, she shrugged it off and said to never tell anyone about it—just like my "cursed gifts." It wasn't until high school, when I heard boys joking, as they do, about sexual acts, that I turned sick and pale with the realization that these acts were part of that "game." There was also another game—a tag team from my grandma and aunt—that involved me getting beaten with belts and meter sticks, dragged by my hair, getting my head plunged in the toilet, or being forced to kneel on rice for hours – these, the consequences for accidentally breaking a glass, losing an earring they'd forced me to wear or getting a "Very Good" instead of "Excellent" on my report cards. Enter Abuse.

By ten, I was forced to become a surrogate parent to my aunt's two young children. I cared for them, waking up at all hours to feed, change diapers, or take them to doctor's visits. When I asked my aunt to get more formula and diapers she'd come home with solid baby food and the wrong size diapers, then blame me for not going to get it myself. Enter the Martyr.

At sixteen, I found out that these same "cousins" were actually my siblings, that my father had raped his wife's sister, and I was the product of that rape. My "aunt" was actually my biological mother.

School was difficult as well. I didn't fit in; I got bullied; I hid my "cursed-gifts" in elementary and used humour to hide the truth during high school. Home life was even worse. At sixteen, I tried living with my parents because I wanted to know what it was like to live in a nuclear family setting. The reality: my father was an addict, a gambler, and extremely abusive, and my mom/aunt forced me to fill some sort of "Cinderella" role.

When I, once an honor student, stopped showing up to class, a concerned school counselor decided to get CFS involved. Believing my father would kill me if the truth got out, I started living on bus routes and becoming familiar with shelters and soup kitchens. One day I went to the convent by the church where I sang, and there a nun showed me the first true acts of kindness, my first hug, and my first "I love you." She helped me get a job, go back to school; she even taught me how to reconcile with my real mother. It didn't last, though, for she later introduced me to her new husband as her "niece."

Finally, I came to the breaking point. What was the point of living? I was bankrupt, a doormat, and learning disabled with "cursed-gifts." Not knowing what love was, I attracted toxic lying cheating partners and friends that manipulated me emotionally, physically and financially. I had health issues: low heart rate, scoliosis, fibromyalgia and migraines that gave me visual auras and even caused me to lose my vision at times. The doctors found a mass in my brain as well, but thankfully I was guided to people who helped me heal and clear it holistically.

It took being on the verge of suicide, before I realized that my experiences were not meant to break me, but to help me help others. That was when my journey of emotional healing truly began.

My medical challenges continued, however, which was not surprising given all the emotional traumas my body endured. Six years ago, I had a heart attack while working out at the gym with my now fiancé (how I met him is another story!). Three years ago, my town had to flee our homes due to wildfires. My accountants filed taxes incorrectly, leaving us with a $200,000 bill. I've lost, over the years, twenty-four loved ones and friends who passed away. All of this while searching for answers to my deteriorating health.

After seeing more than fifteen doctors, enduring countless tests and visits to the ER, being misdiagnosed, rejected for care, and air-vac'd to the city hospital for what turned out to be a failed ablation heart surgery, it became clear that I couldn't be helped in Canada. Some doctors told me I needed a pacemaker, while others told me to accept a decreased quality of life. I went from being physically fit to gaining weight, fainting, barely making it up the stairs, and being bedridden from dizziness, fatigue, and pain. My heart would speed up then drop dramatically, meaning I'd go from feeling fine one minute to completely discombobulated the next.

Eventually, I found a doctor from England who would change everything. Just this past month we discovered I don't require heart surgery after all. All my symptoms were pointing to Dysautonomia, a malfunction of the nervous system that causes, among other things, heart problems. This past November, I found another doctor in Arizona. Since following his protocol, my allergy to garlic and the sun is nonexistent. According to him, physical trauma isn't the only reason for the body to attack itself, but also the buildup of emotional trauma. Despite all the mental and spiritual healing I had undergone, my physical body still hasn't fully recovered. Enter Loss.

In overcoming these traumas I have learned that blaming our losses on those who failed to protect us doesn't help us heal. Forgiveness does. I've learned doctors don't have all the answers, for they are human too. I've learned that clearings and crystals are useful but don't fix cognitive patterns; conscious work still needs to be done. Finally, I learned that every person plays a part in our stories and family isn't always blood.

Suffering from Rejection, Abuse, Betrayal, Abandonment, Loss, and Neglect gave me the gift of compassion. Hate gave me the gifts of love, generosity, and forgiveness. Lies gave me the gift to see the truth and be authentic. Darkness gave me the opportunity to understand there are also others hiding, hoping to find the light exposing the shadows of shame and misconceptions we imprint with. Our negatively-charged reactions can deplete us and overburden us with guilt, misery, and limitations. I could have chosen to stay stuck two steps in the past (depression) or two steps in the future (anxiety); being in the now is how I took my power back and accepted that each perceived failure was a temporary stumbling on my road to success.

The keys to knowledge can free us, but we still need to learn to use them. My journey to enlightenment was to learn to balance pain and peace, which I did thanks to the work of therapists, sound therapy, retreats, gyms, shamans, healers, hypnotherapists, yogis and more. Resilience pushed me to work in four jobs to support my family while getting my diploma in Business Administration, certifications in holistic modalities, and a Masters in Counseling Psychology.

My experience prepped me to connect with clients who have also endured sexual, physical, and emotional traumas; eating disorders and addictions; infidelity of a partner; grief and loss; and health and financial challenges. Practicing what I preach and being transparent about my challenging, non-linear journey, has helped to inspire others. Everything can have a miracle and everything can be healed; you just have to change your perception.

Along the way I have gained an unconditionally loving brother who makes up for my estrangements, accepting friends, and a loving, patient, supportive fiancé with whom I humbly serve our amazing clients at Infinite Strength, our mind, body, and soul center. This journey enriched me to be more than I was expected to be: a human be-ing with an identity and a voice to advocate for myself and to lead others to love, forgive, have compassion and acceptance, and find their own voice.

ABOUT THE AUTHOR: Anna Trillana is an intuitive clinical counselor/therapist, hypnotherapist, and energy healer whose purpose is to teach others to deal with their daily demands and personal crises with compassion, acceptance, and integrity. Anna and her fiancé Andrew are the co-owners of Infinite Strength, a mind, body, and soul center located in Fort McMurray, Alberta and serving clients everywhere. As a movement specialist and nutritionist, Andrew grounds Anna's evolving integration of Counseling, Hypnotherapy, Embodied work (Reiki, IET, MDS, SRT, Qi Gong, Yoga), Sound Therapy, and more. Together, they work with individuals, groups, and couples of all ages, promoting understanding and healing of the past and present by instilling seeds of self-awareness and self-love.

Anna Trillana
Infinite Strength ~ infinitestrength.ca
info@infinitestrength.ca ~ 587-645-0880
@infintestrength.ca (Instagram) ~ @infinitestrngth (Twitter)
facebook.com/infinitestrength

Choose Love
Hillory Hanson

My conscious journey into authenticity began when I was in my thirties. I had been born into a very protective and extremely structured religious family in a small town in British Columbia. It wasn't until I had moved away from home that I started questioning my beliefs and their foundations. I started searching for my truth.

Along the way I heard that humans are motivated into action by two things: love or fear. I don't recall where I heard that statement but it changed my life. I made a conscious decision to choose love as much as I could, which for me meant leaving my faith. I knew that in making this decision, I risked losing everything I held dear to my heart, including my blood and spiritual families, yet I also could not deny that practicing my religion amplified fear. I chose love and stepped into my truth, hoping for the best. While I did lose my family and my childhood religious tribe no longer spoke to me, what I gained exceeded my wildest imagination and desires.

One day I found myself at a psychic fair, where I received a reading that changed the direction of my life. The psychic looked like a little Romanian gypsy, with dyed red hair and tiny hands with pointy red fingernails. She had a smoker's cough and a voice like a whisky drinker. She asked me if I realized I was psychic too. "No," I replied "I don't think so." I'd always been really good at reading people's body language, had good street smarts, but psychic? No way! She asked me to cut the deck of regular playing cards that she used to perform her readings and divide it into four piles. I did as I was told without giving it much thought. She looked at me, then began counting the cards in each pile. Each pile had thirteen cards in it. I had cut that deck evenly without even trying! That got my attention!

After that reading, I started exploring the truth about my spiritual gifts. I purchased a deck of divination cards and started doing readings for myself and anyone willing to play with me. It felt natural, authentic, and loving to me and I felt a spiritual connection to my guides and angels that I had never experienced before. I also enjoyed being of assistance to others and bringing more clarity into their lives or validating things they had been experiencing that were out of the realm of "normal." It was full circle for me!

Later that year I would have another experience that would dramatically change the course of my life. It was a hot weekend, and I was visiting Nelson, British Columbia when I quite unexpectedly fell in love with a woman. And I fell *hard*. In that moment, my world, and all the ideas I had held about "who I was" were completely shattered. Was I straight? What did I really know about myself? I now had to make that decision again—choose fear, and stay where I was comfortable, or choose love and risk the unknown in order to be true to myself. I chose love. I discovered that for me, love is spirit recognizing spirit, no matter what form they happen to be in at the time. If I hadn't allowed myself to explore my own sexuality, I would never have found my true soul mate.

I had kidded that I was a lazy soul and would have planned for my soul mate to live next door to me, not on the other side of the world. Little did I know how right I was!

I had moved to the Okanagan because I felt like I'd meet my soul mate there. That's where I reconnected with Janet, who was in town visiting her dad. Though Janet and I had grown up down the street from each other, we hadn't seen each other in more than fifteen years. The connection was immediate, powerful, and for me, terrifying. I knew what she was thinking, felt her physical pain, and felt her emotions. She was also in a long term relationship with a man. Dare I share my true feelings with a straight woman, and a very special friend? Janet was another love choice I had made, and the one I consider responsible for my very survival.

Fast forward a couple of years. Due to genetic predisposition, malformed intestines, and luck, I ended up going on another life-altering journey. I had been not feeling well for a couple of months, and finally, when I could no longer endure the pain and discomfort, I told Janet I wanted to go to the emergency room. After a cursory exam and recommendation that I get an ultrasound done of my belly the doctor sent me home. That wasn't good enough for Janet, who immediately drove me to a medical imaging facility in Airdrie, a city a half-hour away. They were about to close but took pity on us and squeezed me in. The technician discovered some issues, took some pictures, wrote a letter, and sent us immediately another thirty minutes down the road to a large hospital in Calgary. Upon arrival I was whisked through the emergency, placed in a room, and tested for all sorts of things. I don't remember a lot about those days except being very hot and feverish. Janet called my estranged family and they came to sit with me while we waited for the diagnosis. I was having a diverticulitis attack but my symptoms were confusing the doctors. After a few weeks I had a sudden pain hit my chest, so severe I felt I was going to die. The doctors discovered liquid had pushed up around my lungs and heart. My intestines had burst. I was rushed into emergency surgery.

Before putting me under anesthesia, the doctors asked my permission to give me blood transfusions. The thought terrified me. I had a hard enough time empathically picking up on other people's emotions from across the room, let along having their blood and DNA running through my veins! I asked them to please if they could, find another way to keep me alive, but if the choice came down to death or a transfusion—I choose life! I knew this was yet another decision that would upset my family: and they didn't even know Janet and I were a couple yet. Things were certainly getting real!

The next two and a half weeks were hell. First, I almost died during surgery. The only blood pressure I had were the liquids they were pumping into my body. Later I would learn the doctors had prepared Janet and my family for my demise. I was then placed in a medically-induced coma to buy my body some time to heal and to fight the numerous infections I had. People assume that those in a coma are sleeping peacefully; this was not the case for me. I was surrounded by darkness and have never felt so afraid and vulnerable in all my life. I had no way to protect or help myself, I had no control, and I knew that it could go either way…live or die! I went through dreamlike tests and experiences. I was tortured physically. I was kidnapped. I worried that Janet couldn't find me and that we'd never be together again. I dreamt of sacrificing my life for my sister and her children. I dreamt of sacrificing my life for all women and children. I passed some tests and failed a few too!

Ten days into the coma, Janet told my ICU nurse that I was a medium and sensitive to dead people so she shouldn't be alarmed if my heart rate fluctuated a lot. She then went out to run an errand. Sure enough, my heart-rate suddenly shot through the roof. Normally they would have immediately given me medications to lower it, but the nurse remembered what Janet had said and decided to wait. What she didn't know was that a woman who had just died on the same floor had pushed me out of my body! I felt such relief in being released from this life. It was as if I had lost five hundred pounds of karma. I felt free! As I floated away, I was thinking how this woman would really enjoy my body. Then it hit me that I was not ready to leave and I thought, "Oh, hell no!" I kicked her spirit out and reconnected myself to the Earth's crystalline grid. I was back! I chose to live! I chose love! I would not leave Janet! A flash of images, my future life and contracts, passed before my eyes, but I retained none of them. The next thing I remember is my sister's voice. She was telling me I had had two surgeries. I was awake! I was back!

The experience taught me a valuable lesson about myself—I had always known, what I was willing to die for—my family, my lovers and my faith, but I had never considered what or whom I'd be willing to live for. Now I knew I would stay for love. I stayed for Janet and for myself!

Coming home from the hospital was hard for everyone. My estranged family went back to their estrangement. I lost them all over again. I had post traumatic stress disorder, and fatigue so severe I sometimes lacked the strength to stand; I also had a huge scar and an ostomy bag to deal with. My short-term memory seemed to have deserted me and I couldn`t remember what I had been told a second earlier. My emotions were all over the place and I would suddenly be triggered into violent anger, grief, or overwhelm. Worst of all, I had to rely on others to help me. Life would never be the same!

It has been a long recovery both physically and emotionally. I had to work through the feelings and self judgment that I had let my health get that critical. I had to reinvent myself, my home, and spiritual life. It took a few years, but I found a wonderful healing support team, who aided me immeasurably in my recovery. One night in a dream I was given the inspiration to develop a line of Bach Flower Remedies. Creating these formulas took me out of my painful story and reignited my passion for exploration and finding my truth. Indeed, the "Faery Heart Elixirs" have helped me with the: overwhelm, anxiety, and fatigue, I struggled with daily. I also found that they helped other sensitive beings on this planet to enjoy more peace, love, and evolutionary support. I traveled all over Alberta and British Columbia sharing them to financially support myself. I also began doing psychic readings again, and found I still loved connecting people back to their own gifts, abilities, and the truth about who they are. This work fed my soul, assisted others, and provided me the freedom to accommodate my fluctuating physical stamina.

Saying yes to this new career path was another non-traditional choice, but again, being true to myself has paid off in spades! I have a wealth of new family and friends, people who are also striving to express their own authenticity. I have a divine purpose that brings me peace and fills me up. I am enjoying more life and more love than ever! I love myself and the magical adventure that is my life!

The work of becoming authentic is never done. It is fluid and changing from moment to moment. For me, fear has never completely gone away. Yet I remain committed to further embodying my big beautiful authentic self, discovering and unearthing more and more of my own gifts and helping others do the same. When I am feeling scared I remember, I always have a choice, fear or love. I choose love!

ABOUT THE AUTHOR: A multidimensional channeler and energy worker, Hillory has been providing clarity, insight, healing, validation, connection, and mentorship through her faery oracle sessions for over fifteen years. Hillory has also created a vibrational line of Faery Heart Elixirs (Bach Flower Remedies) that assists herself and other sensitive beings, emotionally and energetically, in enjoying more peace, love, support, and protection in their everyday lives and throughout their evolution. She is passionate about helping others awaken to their unique gifts and shares a wealth of knowledge, unique perspectives, and a vast love that makes for an enlightening and empowering experience for those who work with her.

Hillory Hanson
Universal Embodiment
universalembodiment.com
inspirationhh@gmail.com
403-819-7502

Purely Embracing Energies that Serve the True Self
The Journey of One Wounded Healer
Laera Morrow

In order to understand the messages the Universe has for us, we must first be open to receiving them. It took years of struggling with epilepsy, and viewing my life as dis-eased because of it, before I finally chose to perceive my life as positive. In doing so, I let go of energetic blockages I'd been carrying and was then able to receive the answer I'd been seeking. I also discovered my path as a natural and energy healer.

During my freshman year of high school, I began suffering from unpredictable spells of zoning out that snuck up on me out of the blue. The diagnosis—"intractable" epilepsy—was not easy to accept, but I soon found relief through anti-epilepsy drugs (AEDs). Later, I was able to quit AEDs altogether, and by the time I started college, I thought seizures were a thing of the past.

As an Anthropology major, I found the most value in studying the different ways through which various human cultures tend to the same basic human needs. Cultural differences aside, one thing globally agreed upon is that *health* ranks at the top of the list of those basic needs. So, I began envisioning a doctorate in Medical Anthropology on the horizon.

First, however, I wanted to vacation from the bubble of academia and milk the real world of all its wisdom before committing to any career path. Not long after earning my bachelor's degree, I moved to Brooklyn, New York. Had I been asked at the time, I would have stayed indefinitely. Finding a decent medical writing gig upon my arrival made particularly smooth sailing of settling into the Big Apple, and my inner anthropologist soon was happy to be studying comedy, bartending at a Harlem dive, and integrating myself into the surrounding community of artisans in Bushwick.

I was soaking up the city that never sleeps—in more ways than I even realized. (This reality was easy to overlook because I was no stranger to feeling *on* by default, thanks to years of playground duels settled by survival of the *wittest*, erudite analyses generating academic accolades, and an overall heightened awareness of my surroundings for survival purposes. I didn't realize how entrenched in my left brain I had become over the years. I was imbalanced.) I'd always known I was a sensitive soul, but didn't fully understand just what that meant. However, it turns out that for an empath to inhabit a city so densely populated while avoiding the inadvertent absorption of surrounding energies requires some focused spiritual strengthening, and that was work that I had yet to do.

Looking back, it's no surprise that it was while living in New York that I experienced my first-ever grand mal seizure, though at the time it knocked me on my ass in more ways than one. The headiness that had brought me positive feedback throughout my life had also led me to lose touch with the energetic focal points throughout my being—including my Root chakra, with all its grounding stability that enables a person to hold their own in the eye of a storm.

It should also have come as no surprise that the AEDs I took in response led to an exponential increase in those ass-knockings. Growing up, I had become incredulous of how the advertising exploits of pharmaceutical companies—in which they celebrated their latest "innovation" while glossing over the risks—remained legal. More recently, my work as a medical writer had enlightened me to the startlingly low standards often maintained throughout pharmaceutical research. More than once, my gut had interrupted my own research to question the morality of the work I was doing. It had been far too easy, though, to turn a blind eye ("I'm just a writer, what do I know?") and pivot my attention to the bustling city around me.

That's when my seizures reappeared.

I did what I knew how to do and got a prescription for the same AEDs I'd taken in high school. However, filling that prescription proved to be a hard lesson in trusting my intuition; I felt a tangible pang in my gut when the pharmacist handed me a pill bottle bearing a different name—*Levetiracetam*. Upon my questioning this discrepancy, she asserted that it was "the same thing". The pang I felt didn't subside, but I chose to swallow the pill—handed to me by the white-lab-coat-wearing professional—anyway.

Sure enough, my seizures skyrocketed. Within the fortnight, I was averaging three grand mals per day, attributable to the one new variable factor in my life—Levetiracetam. I later learned that the same generic AED had worsened the condition of many other epileptics, and that class action lawsuits were underway.

> *The Universe first whispers to us. . . If we do not hear, it taps us lightly on the head. . . If we continue to ignore it, it pounds on our gateway. . . Eventually, if that does not elicit a proper invitation, the Universe whacks us on the crown, knocks us out, and barges in.*

And, *whacked* I had been! I didn't know what to do about my worsening condition, but I begrudgingly admitted that blacking out on my way to catch the 2am L train did *not* sound appealing. So I left New York and headed to Portland, Oregon. A good friend had once told me I would dig the place, and in light of my recent experiences, the city's allegedly easygoing pace and thriving holistic medicine scene sounded especially inviting.

I spent the first two years in my new home on a mission to remedy my health. I struck up new relationships with both specialty epileptologists and alternative practitioners. I tried neurofeedback therapy, ketogenic dieting, acupuncture, and AEDs a, b, c, d, x, y, and

z. Nothing quashed my seizures, though, and because mine were so frequent, my brain never got a chance to fully recover. I was living in a constant postictal state (the mental fog that comes after a seizure's shock to the nervous system, which can last anywhere from seconds to a fortnight, and can bring its own entire slew of complications). The only light at the end of the tunnel was Oregon's impending legalization of medical cannabis. I was thrilled to finally get some into my hands, only to find that it didn't stop the daily seizures.

Eventually, I gave up hope of escaping this perpetual cycle of seizure and fog. Yet, I didn't despair. Instead I chose to accept—and even *embrace*—the hand I had been dealt in life. Logically, I couldn't see anything else left *to* do (I'd tried everything shy of brain surgery, and *that* wasn't happening anytime soon). Postictalness was an impaired state of consciousness, but, I decided, it didn't have to be an unhappy one.

One day, I walked into my local natural grocery store, looked up at the chilled shelf bearing a bounty of kombucha flavors, and I had an epiphany: Yes, I'd had plans for my life, and they didn't include paying for my groceries with food stamps or otherwise surviving on Disability payments. But the fact was that I *was* surviving. In fact, I was outright *living*, and on gourmet organic foods at that. Meanwhile, some folks were just biding their time until retirement so they could start living. In that moment I realized I'd been taking for granted everything I actually *did* have, and it was time I muster up some gratitude for it.

Suddenly, a tangible weight lifted from my shoulders, and I was able, finally, to stop desperately grasping for a cure to my epilepsy. For so long I had seen it as a roadblock to my life, when really, the biggest roadblock had been my own negative energy—and now I had just overcome it!

It's a basic law of quantum physics that *like* attracts *like*. The higher the frequency of an entity, the higher the frequencies that it attracts. Sure enough, the week after I lifted my spirits, the golden treasure that I'd just quit seeking fell into my lap.

It happened during yoga class when—for once—I had a seizure at the right place at the right time. After the class (and the seizure) ended, Sonya, the instructor, approached me and said I needed to apply essential oil of Frankincense to the balls of my feet. This message had just "come to" her (she was also a shamanic conduit).

I was skeptical, to say the least. To my rational brain, Sonya seemed like a "Mary Kay" type, prepared as she was with a sales kit full of supplies. Besides, I'd already tried everything under the sun, and now this lady was telling me that oil on my feet would make the difference? Not to mention, I was busy reveling in my newfound lack of concern for whether or not a difference *would* ever *be* made.

My gut was picking up good vibes, though. First and foremost, Sonya was genuine. I could tell that she actually *wanted* to help me out, which was a pleasant change from the numerous "healthcare" professionals who, given their aloof demeanor and disregard for my input, obviously didn't *care* about me *or* my *health*.

If I'd learned anything by that point, it was to *not* ignore my gut. I had nothing to lose by taking her advice, anyway. I accepted the free sample of Frankincense being offered to me, and lightheartedly began my new daily regimen of podiatric oil application, sans hopes or expectations.

Eureka! To my astonishment, *it worked*. By the next month, my seizures had decreased from thrice per day to once per week (no other treatments involved), and continued to decrease.

It turns out that Frankincense has been known as "the king of oils" for centuries in the Middle East. Moreover, in ayurvedic medicine, Frankincense is regarded as an incredible healing herb that is particularly beneficial for brain health, and is known to foster *groundedness*—precisely what I'd been lacking. Somehow, though, years of Catholic schooling had failed to teach me the actual value of the Wise Men's gift, and countless neurologists had failed to inform me that it could far surpass pharmaceuticals in effectiveness. My firsthand experience with the power of natural medicine inspired me to spread some much-needed awareness of it. I was impassioned to take action—*and I was finally capable of doing so!*

Meanwhile, my firsthand experiences with unseen energies (tangible sensations; undeniable synchronicities; solutions channeled from other dimensions) inspired me to study energy medicine. Ultimately, through learning to manipulate energies and communicate with realms beyond the third dimension, I found my passion in healing work, and ultimately, the way to living as my best, authentic self.

We must invest in our personal health so that we are *capable* of investing our energies elsewhere. Though there is a time and a place for allopathic medicine, it far too often neglects to expose underlying causes of chronic health problems and instead settles for masking symptoms with long-term pharmaceutical treatment (with all of its risks), and resorts to labeling problems it can't solve as "intractable". Such a "healthcare" system is *prolonging sickness*, not *promoting health*.

Personal health is based in the physical, spiritual, mental, and emotional realms of being. Holistic healthcare recognizes the interconnectedness of these realms, is geared toward unearthing root causes of health problems, and employs natural and energy medicines. *Why would it* not *be our default mode of healthcare?*

I also founded a healing business, based upon the following truths:
- Health is our most vital investment as humans—on both the personal and societal scales.
- Our spiritual, mental, emotional, and physical health is all interrelated. (*Like* frequencies attract *like* frequencies.)
- *Success* is measured by *happiness*, which is only a sidestep away. (*Now* is the time.)
- To consciously know the *True Self*, one must first recognize the accumulated masks shielding oneself from their own eyes.
- True healing requires 3 R's: *recognize* the problem, *release* negative energies causing it, and *receive* positive energy.

- Listen for patterns in your life. If you hear anything…keep listening. (The Universe is knocking.)
- The gut is wiser than the brain. (Trust it.)

Natural and energy medicine: if it's good enough for Jesus, it's good enough for me.

ABOUT THE AUTHOR: Laera Morrow is a holistic healer, speaker, writer, and owner of Laera's Lair of Natural Healing. She heals clients living with brain and nerve dis-ease by using natural and energy medicine to identify and treat the root causes of health issues. Laera lives in Portland, Oregon, where she serves her community as a Reiki Master, wellness coach, shamanic practitioner, and essential oils consultant. Currently, she is continuing her studies at the LightSong School of 21st Century Shamanism and Energy Medicine. Laera is also a singer, songwriter, and violinist who circulates her message through her music along with her band of fellow shamanic healers and conduits.

Laera Morrow
Laera's Lair of Natural Healing
laeraslair.com
laera@laeraslair.com
501-580-2886

Learning to Live Like Kathy
Rebecca Egan

One lovely day in 2014, I was driving down the hilly streets of Point Loma, San Diego and staring in awe at the palm trees rising to great heights in the overcast sky. A warm gentle breeze was blowing my hair from my face as my convertible MINI Cooper cruised past the library with kids running around out front; the church, with streams of people who flowed onto the steps after mass; a coffee shop with locals and their dogs enjoying the midmorning calm.

Suddenly, I felt the urge to call my mom. She picked up on the first ring, always eager to hear my voice across the miles. Several months earlier, Ryan, my boyfriend of four years, and I had packed up our belongings and our dog and drove the nearly three thousand miles from Massachusetts to Southern California. Neither of us had jobs, but we trusted that everything would fall into place. And it had. There was no shortage of nursing jobs, and I was soon working at a nearby hospital.

As on our previous phone calls, I told Mom about the beauty and ease of living in San Diego; how people really enjoyed life, rather than rushing about, ticking off items on their to-do lists. "Mom, everyone here just seems much happier than back home." I paused. "But that's not why I'm calling… I had kind of a crazy idea. I know I don't practice yoga much, but I keep getting this feeling that I should do a yoga teacher training." I went on to explain what a YTT entailed, and the nagging feeling I couldn't shake. Though I had only been to four or five classes, I had the sense that it could change me fundamentally, or at least teach me more about myself.

"Beck, it sounds like a great idea," Mom replied, "Only positivity can come from immersing yourself in a practice you're passionate about. I think you should do it."

I breathed a sigh of relief. If Mom thought I should put myself out there then she was probably right. She had always been my biggest cheerleader, living somewhat vicariously through me and encouraging me to seize every opportunity. I told her I was going to a class that night to meet the studio owner and lead teacher of YTT.

After the class I signed up immediately. Something about the soothing space and the welcoming people called to me. The way I felt lying there on my mat, breathing in subtle calming scents and taking a moment of peace for myself. It all nudged me gently, like someone tapping on my shoulder. "You need this," it seemed to say.

One month later, I was headed home after a grueling twelve-hour shift on an oncology floor and looking forward to spending some quality time with Ryan. We spent hours that night watching one of those shows about tiny houses and dreaming about what our future would look like. We playfully toyed with the idea of building a community of tiny houses that we could talk our friends and parents into joining. Finally, we climbed into bed, tired but still happily chatting about all the possibilities ahead of us.

I woke up the next morning to thirty missed calls and many missed texts from my dad and brother, all telling me to call home immediately.

"What's going on?" I said when Dad answered, my heart pounding in my ears. Through tears and with devastating sadness in his voice, he said, "Beck you need to sit down. Your mom died. I found her dead in the bathroom this morning." I could hear him quietly crying but sound was drowned out by my own sobs.

"What? No…No, Dad. Mom can't be dead. She can't be. Not Mom. I talked to her yesterday. No. Dad she was my best friend. What am I going to do without her?"

I then asked myself the question I didn't want to say out loud: *Had my mother killed herself?*

My mind flashed back to another phone call five months before. My dad had called to tell me Mom was back in the hospital. She hadn't attempted suicide again, but she felt unsafe home alone. She was admitted to safely alter her medications and receive intensive therapy.

I don't remember walking into my room, but that's where Ryan found me, curled up into myself on the end of the bed.

"I'm here, Beck," he said as he wrapped his arms around my shivering body. "I'm so sorry."

The strangest thoughts were running through my mind as overwhelming despair engulfed me. Dad tried to reassure me that everything would be okay; he also said he couldn't be sure of the cause of death but it didn't seem like suicide.

The next day I was back in Massachusetts, but without Mom, it no longer felt like home. She would never again call out to me as I walked through the door. I wouldn't get to hear her silly mom jokes said in the worst accents. I immediately walked into their bathroom and sat on the floor where she died, resting my palms on the cold tile.

The next few days were a blur. My brother and I wrote her obituary and helped Dad make the arrangements. We were amazed at how many of Mom's high school friends showed up, along with people we'd known from childhood, and family from near and far.

There wasn't a dry eye among them as I delivered her eulogy. Laughter surrounded me as I recounted her dressing up as a cat at a Halloween party she didn't know was only for kids. Everyone nodded along when I told about how adults and children alike loved Kathy Libby and could chat with her for hours.

In the months that followed I replayed the day she died on an endless loop in my mind. I kept wondering if it wouldn't have happened if I were there. The past eight months of San Diego bliss had dissolved into regret.

Yet something remarkable happened when Ryan and I returned, something that lit up the endless darkness. The community we had built in San Diego nurtured us, bringing us food, gifts, and plants. The women of the yoga studio listened, showed genuine sympathy, and held space for me. Their care was unwavering even though I knew at times it was uncomfortable for them.

Though I missed my mother terribly and always would, a realization began to settle over me. By being the positive loving person she was, she had guided me to the ideal place to have all the support I needed. By encouraging me to take what many thought of as an expensive and unnecessary chance, she surrounded me with people who, like her, showed me unconditional love. They carried me through a time when I had become completely ungrounded without my mother to tether me to the earth.

Through the support of others, movement and meditation, and a diet of whole live foods, I healed more each day. I continued to learn about the yogic lifestyle, which seeks to unite all parts of the self. I began delving deeply into myself and my family, and gradually aligned myself to live as authentically as possible. I was able to connect to my true self more easily, and to see our connection with one another. This introspection, forced upon me by the loss of my mother, catapulted me towards a deeper understanding of the kind of healer and nurturer I was.

I began to listen to my body, and to pay attention to my thoughts and patterns. What was my self-talk like? How was that affecting me? I also began really listening to others, instead of always being in my head trying to formulate a response to ensure I didn't sound "idiotic."

It was the beginning of an awakening that would continue over the next four years. I said yes to opportunities I probably wouldn't have in the past. I took courses in various energy modalities to learn to heal the people I loved, including myself, more effectively. My learning was always in the spirit of my mother. I asked myself constantly what she would tell me to do and the answer was always the same: Follow your intuition.

When Ryan said he thought we should move back to Massachusetts, I reluctantly agreed. San Diego had taught me more about myself, and how to live authentically, than I ever expected. I was changed to my very core.

What had truly changed me, I knew, were the people, the experiences, and the willingness to look beyond the norm or the mainstream. What changed me was the deep heartache that kept me up at night, the worry that I hadn't told Mom enough that I loved her and was proud of her. We talked all the time, but had I really listened?

I vowed. I vowed to never feel that way again and to live in the spirit of my mom. I vowed to make conversation with strangers and to have empathy. I vowed to listen deeply to others, past the words to hear what they didn't know they were saying. I vowed to remember every day that she wasn't here and I was.

We made our return trip back east into a vacation, stretching it over two weeks and more than five thousand miles. The last leg of our journey turned into a race to beat a Nor'easter, which we did with mere hours to spare. Our arrival home was a bit of a whirlwind, both figuratively and literally. In the midst of a snowstorm and preparations for my dad's sixtieth birthday party, Ryan and I found out I was pregnant.

A high school friend posted on social media about using a local home birth midwife. My curiosity piqued, I called and scheduled an appointment to see if her vision of birth matched ours.

Ryan and I instantly loved the midwife. We felt calmed, heard, and validated in her presence, and she soon felt like a trusted friend. When I called to tell her I was bleeding, she suggested drawing labs, and later compassionately broke the news that I was miscarrying. A few months later I conceived again, and though I was still heartbroken about the miscarriage, I couldn't help but be in awe that my baby was now due on my dad's birthday, the same day I was due to be born. I also knew that as long as I trusted my body, my midwife, and felt supported I would have the home birth experience I desired. Nature would do its job with very little intervention necessary.

Nine thrilling yet exhausting months later, I got my wish. Olive Rose entered the world peacefully, surrounded by family in the same house my mother died in. That point was important to me. Even though many people were uncomfortable with the idea of home birth, they all agreed with the notion of coming full circle and changing the energy of the house. Now as I looked around, I didn't just see and feel the heavy weight of my mom's death. I was reminded of the joy of birthing my baby at home.

I have found authenticity to be an ever-changing principle that I'm constantly reassessing and working towards. These days, it is being aware of my self-talk so as to be the best role model for my daughter. Being present and in the moment as she discovers the feel of fresh cut green grass on her tiny bare feet. Stepping into her perspective as she gazed around in wonder while seeing snow for the first time. Reminding myself to laugh with her about something silly instead of curling into myself with worry over tomorrow or next year. To push to always be better for her and consider the impact my actions are having on shaping her future. And to always remember to follow my intuition. The world outside of us has a way of complicating our original intention through suggestion or competition. I have found that if I come back to center, my true intention for any situation is usually based in love. And love has never steered me wrong.

ABOUT THE AUTHOR: Rebecca Egan is a Registered Nurse, Reiki practitioner, certified yoga teacher, ThetaHealing® Practitioner, Quantum Touch practitioner, and wellness blogger. She was always committed to the health and wellbeing of others, but it was after the unexpected death of her mother that she began walking her spiritual path. Rebecca's passion lies in learning how best to serve her community in whole body wellness and using integrative medicine to bridge the disparities in healthcare. She is currently studying herbalism, nutrition, and taking courses at University of Arizona Center for Integrative Medicine. Rebecca lives in Massachusetts with her husband, father, daughter, three dogs, and seven chickens!

Rebecca Egan RN, BSN
Certified Yoga Teacher, Reiki Level II Practitioner
oliveandom.com
bekkaegan@gmail.com

Becoming
Andrea Fesler

Have you ever wondered how one comes to live authentically? It's not as if you wake up one day with light shining down from the heavens and start twirling around, all light and joyful and screaming from the top of your lungs, "Look at me, everyone! I am now my authentic self!"

I'll admit I have often wished it was that simple. However, I have come to realize that the beauty of authenticity is that it is an unending process that requires courage and constant action. The first step is to figure out who we truly are, which in and of itself is a lengthy process of questioning, self-discovery, unbecoming, and rediscovery. As we evolve, so does the truth of our authentic nature. Each day we have new experiences that serve to teach us and allow us to expand—physically, emotionally, and spiritually. Each moment we get to choose to respond in a way that aligns with who we are or are in the process of becoming.

For me, bearing witness to the suffering of others has offered the greatest lessons on authentic living. As a nurse working in hospice, oncology, and bone marrow transplant for over eighteen years, I have walked with thousands of people facing terminal illness. Some of them have successful treatments and go forward to have longer, more fulfilling lives. More of them die, leave their bodies, and get to start again. Their journeys have empowered me to change my own life.

Through my patients, I have learned that death is not something to be feared, but rather embraced as a normal part of the lifecycle. In fact, when a person and his/her family are properly prepared and have had a chance to work through their unfinished business, death is one of the most beautiful, deeply healing experiences we can have.

The most spectacular energy I have ever experienced is when a departing soul releases from the body and is greeted by ancestors, angels, guides, and God. It is in this moment, as they are being ushered home, that these souls shower those left behind with an indescribable amount of unconditional love, leaving with us the energy that we need to continue our journey here.

I first felt this energy two weeks after experiencing an intuitive awakening. On my second day working as a nurse in home hospice, I received a call from a nursing home that one of the patients was actively dying. As I opened the door to the facility I was bombarded by the stale smell of must and mothballs and the frantic energy of the staff. I did my best to quell their fears, then headed to Evelyn's room. The other nurses had told me her daughter was on the way, but at that moment Evelyn was alone.

Due to the nature of my work, I had developed a heightened sense of awareness, especially regarding death. Indeed, when I entered Evelyn's room, it was like stepping out of the nursing home and into another dimension. I could feel the presence of death permeating every atom of it. Yet the space felt light, and the scent of roses wafted in and out of my awareness, replacing the unpleasant smell that had greeted me at the entrance. Waves of warmth and tingles would periodically come in through the top of my head and flood down my body. In my peripheral vision I could see twinkling lights, indicating to me the presence of her angels and guides there to welcome her soul home.

As this was my first time meeting Evelyn, I took my time surveying her body and performing my clinical assessment. I watched her chest rise and fall, felt her cool wrist and noted the weak pulse, and carefully observed her face looking for signs of pain, of which there were none. The skin on her forehead was soft and relaxed, and a peaceful presence surrounded her body, reminding me of gentle snow falling from the sky on a cool winter's day. I then scanned the room, gathering information to get a sense of who Evelyn was.

From the hundreds of photos of family and friends scattered about I could tell she was a loved and cherished matriarch. She also had frequent visits from her family, as her clothes were clean, labeled with her name, and hung meticulously in her closet. In the corner of her closet she had a personal supply of expensive adult diapers and soft baby wipes, rather than the economical brand used at the facility. On her dresser sat bottles of French perfume, a gold-plated hand-held mirror, powder, night cream, bobby pins, and bright red lipstick. I imagined her sitting at the vanity, pinning up her hair and applying lipstick. She struck me as the kind of woman who found a way to enjoy life, no matter the circumstance.

Even now, as she was about to depart this world, I could feel the warmth of her love radiating from her heart. This love, cultivated throughout her life, was present and assisting in the release from her body. Suddenly I heard the rate of her breathing change and knew her final breaths were near. I walked over to her bedside and held her hand, weathered and wrinkled from a lifetime of experiences. I knelt down and whispered in her ear, "It's okay to go, Evelyn, you've lived a beautiful life." Just as I stood up again her daughter walked through the door. I ushered her over to her mother's bedside and, three breaths later, Evelyn was gone.

What happened next, nothing could have prepared me for. As it released from her body, her soul showered down wave after wave of the most loving, highest vibrational energy I have ever felt. I would have fallen to my knees had it not been for the chair behind me. For twenty minutes I sat in complete silence, holding her daughter's hand and basking in the love of Evelyn washing over us as she was transforming. The love and the bliss I felt filled me up so much it had to release, with silent tears trickling down my cheeks. Though her daughter and I did not speak, I could tell she was experiencing the same feelings.

Not all the deaths I have witnessed have been this beautiful. I have found that people who have lived inauthentically and without processing difficult life experiences have a much more difficult time releasing from their bodies. It is as if the Universe is with us our entire lives, gently nudging us to look at our issues and deal with them, and when we ignore these messages we end up with disease in our bodies and our minds. If our unwillingness to evolve and progress goes on long enough, the Universe's whisper turns to a loud roar, an earthquake bringing down the foundation we thought we had created. On our deathbed nothing is left unseen, unfelt, or unfinished. The earlier we are able to face ourselves, the more beautiful and meaningfully we can live our lives.

The reality of impending death helps us to get our priorities straight and see what is truly meaningful and important in life. Many of us must feel uncomfortable in order to change, and while facing mortality is certainly a fast track way to that, it doesn't have to be that hard! We don't have to hit bottom or have a terminal illness to become empowered, authentic, and create a life we love; rather, each day gives us an opportunity to choose how easy or difficult we make the process.

I have received so much more wisdom, love, truth, and healing from my patients than I have been able to give to them, and I know that choosing to stay small would dishonor the teachings that have been passed on to me. In order to honor the lives of my patients and in devotion to God, it is my responsibility to constantly heal my life and bring that same healing to others. Each time I journey with someone to the gates of heaven it brings up my own fears and unfinished business and gives me the opportunity to examine and work through them. Healing is like unraveling a ball of yarn; sometimes you can't see what is inside until you have freed the layers on the top. We are not meant to suffer and there is supreme happiness for us if we are willing to do the work. The work is not always easy, but it is always worth it.

Witnessing the authenticity of death gave me strength to become a nurse, overcome the trauma of childhood sexual abuse, overcome addictions, leave an unhealthy marriage, leave my hometown when

I was being stalked and the restraining order failed to protect me, repair damaged relationships, and free myself from relationships that were toxic. Again, the work was not easy, and at my lowest point I decided drastic change was necessary for my survival. I became a traveling nurse and for seven years I moved about the country, never remaining in one place for more than three months. I discovered so much beauty in the world and, as the world opened up to me, I opened up to myself. I took an assignment in San Diego, where I had an intuitive awakening after an energy healing session. It was then that I realized there was more to my life's purpose than being a nurse, that all the experiences up to that moment were preparing me to step into a larger version of myself. It was then I understood that there had been a divine purpose for my suffering; it was what it took to get me to see the truth.

For the next year I took as many classes as I could in order to learn how to manage my newly discovered abilities, and how to heal myself, as I too had illnesses at that time. I remember being in my first healing class and feeling energy in my body and my teacher providing me with the words to express what was happening. I kept thinking, *How could all of this even be possible, and why didn't anyone tell me sooner?*

As amazed and awestruck as I was, I also had a lot of fear around following my new calling. My family couldn't understand me anymore; some friends and my partner of three years fell out of my life. This beautiful gift of intuition and healing I had been given also required me to step into a more authentic version of myself. I experienced a complete overhaul of my life, both internally and externally. There were times I doubted myself, my abilities, and even my sanity. In those dark times, it was always my patients' experiences that comforted me and gave me hope.

Walking with death these many years has taught me more about living than anything else could. The relationships cultivated at the end of life are sacred and deep. There is no more time for masks or walls, and vulnerability and authenticity become essential to the soul's survival. When I felt discouraged or uncertain about my gifts, I would think about the regrets they had confided in me. I didn't want to be on my deathbed one day, regretting that I had ignored God's call to follow my spiritual path. Besides, if my patients could find the strength necessary to face death, I could most certainly find the strength to be different.

Becoming different from my peers and stepping outside of the paradigm I had been conditioned to be in, was not and still is not, always easy. I call upon God with every breath and I never forget the divine lessons learned from my patients. Their experiences have given me the courage to be the best, most authentic version of me.

ABOUT THE AUTHOR: Andrea Fesler is a Registered Nurse, Medical Intuitive, and ThetaHealing® Master Instructor and Practitioner. She has worked in oncology, bone marrow transplant, and hospice for eighteen years. After discovering her intuitive abilities, she became certified in multiple energy healing modalities and trained as an End of Life Doula through the International End of Life Doula Association (INELDA). Andrea lives in Colorado Springs, where she has an energy healing, teaching, and end of life doula practice. She also works once a week as an oncology nurse and is an active member of Toastmasters International. Her passion lies in bridging the gap between the medical and holistic worlds to mainstream alternative healing.

Andrea Fesler
Energy With Andrea
energywithandrea.com
info@energywithandrea.com
619-247-8089

Consider the Beauty of Honesty
As a Lead-in to Authenticity by Way of Vulnerability
Ruthe Hanson Plaché

Deciding to pursue an advanced degree in Voice and Sacred Music was pretty predictable for me since I grew up in a home where this would have been a cherished virtue. My parents had a strong dedication and allegiance to ministry and the church and I began singing there at a very early age. Though church music in the Midwest was limiting, I was determined to do as much singing as possible and be a good musician.

My desire to master the art of singing had been ignited when late at night I would lie in bed and listen to classical singers on the radio. It was a very different kind of singing than I was used to, and for sure it wasn't the pop or country music sound. Yet I was mesmerized by their talent and wondered how sound like that was possible. To pursue this dream would certainly require a great deal of tenacity, and I thought I had plenty of that. Little did I know this would be a pathway to embrace honesty and humility and to live vulnerably.

There were already plenty of very good singers in church and my high school and college music classes (the intimidation factor is real!), yet I wondered why I was never given solo spots in choir or musicals. At home there wasn't a lot of encouragement because singing scales and trying to get the voice to flow freely was annoying to my parents and siblings. When I asked to take private lessons I was met with some resistance around cost and transportation issues. Determined to do whatever it took to make it happen, I did chores around the house to pay for lessons and took the bus to the other end of town. Thrilled at having accomplished my goal, I was crushed when my first vocal teacher, after listening to me sing, suggested I find a different form of self-expression. I would never be a singer, he said. I left that day completely dejected. What would I do now?

Hearing unfavorable comments from others—even when well-intentioned and necessary—was a real challenge for my soul. However, I started to question what my teacher had said. If he didn't think I could succeed as a singer, why? What was I doing or not doing that wasn't what he wanted or expected to hear? I knew I had the desire to sing and was determined to find a way in spite of what appeared to be a closed door. I said to myself, "I can do this." Despite his opinion, that teacher agreed to continue working with me, and I began to learn the disciplines, the tools, and the techniques needed to pursue my dream. Yet at the same time I longed to experience the freedom and ease that would allow the voice to grow naturally.

Things shifted somewhat when my dad's brother came for a visit. He was a music teacher with a passion for seeing others enjoy the gift of music as much as he did. Dad asked me to sing for him, probably in the hopes that he would provide some instruction on how to make a more consistent and pleasing sound. My parents had repeatedly made suggestions on what they thought I should sound like or be doing with my voice.

After I sang for my uncle, he smiled and said, "Lie down on the floor. Breathe naturally, feel your breath, relax, now sing the song."

It felt awkward, difficult, unfamiliar. When I finished he presented his theory on natural, free, and melodious singing and encouraged me to continue this kind of exercise until I began to feel comfortable with it and could produce, pure, gentle, natural tone without manipulation or nuance.

Trust me on this one, it's been a lifelong experiment. Listening to input and seeking to engage myself in prescribed new ways was part of this pathway. I had many teachers and studied various genres before finding the music and repertoire that fit my voice. It was about learning to be true to myself, my dream and desire in spite of setbacks, mistakes, criticisms, and others' often conflicting opinions.

I'll be honest: the decision to pursue singing was partly based on a desire to receive recognition; however, there was something else as well. I was responding to a call from an inner voice that said, *Sing, because that's what you love to do.* For sure I experienced a little bit of what feels good and made me happy. There was also the added benefit of the breath work, which is great for general health and the lungs in particular. At the same time the exercises seemed to be more than that. In essence, they provided a very real platform by which I learned to go inside, find the real purpose for the pursuit, be honest with the process, and keep open to the wisdom of tried and true methods from artists who had found their measure of success by not giving up.

My many teachers were an interesting study as well. Each had his/her own ideas of how the voice works best; each had something new to add to the mix when explaining the vocal mechanism and making singing sound. At times it was confusing to figure out how to make sense of all the unique approaches. After an audition with a very fine singer and coach, she said, "Well, Ruth, you make quite a fine noise. I think I can help you learn to sing, but you are older now and have a lot of bad habits." I was thirty-seven at the time but the passion to learn and achieve had never left me. The disciplines of life had revealed that coming home and knowing myself, truly trusting myself, was part of the process of finding the unique inner vibration that was me.

There was also a very important lesson I needed to learn. I had always tried too hard, putting unnecessary effort into most things, especially singing. Teachers would often tell me to "cut the smulch and just sing the message." Boy, it took me a long time to get honest with how I came across, often with pressure in personality as well as pressure on the chords. Neither works in the end.

What I learned through this process of accepting myself was the conscious awareness that when making singing sound it must come from "the zone of the vibration space within me" inside my body. Indeed, like most spiritual practices in life it's an inside job. There is a place from which each person resonates and transmits authenticity. Even the meditation on OM must be felt by the breath descending into the body and being. The singer's authentic vibration, color, and sound is when the tone is internalized. Singing is when the notes and words are sung into the heart and soul. There is no pushing breath out the mouth, in fact tone is all draw into the body, riding on the breath, freely, while vibration happens. The listener can hear it and feel it. The sound must be clear and never waiver from that comfortable, concentrated, magical place of being aligned with self.

The lesson I continue to take away is I must feel something in order to convey it without pretense. The song must *be me*. I must first be able to sing the song to myself and feel the meaning of what I am saying, otherwise it won't be felt by the listener. At the same time it is given freely to the listener with no expectation of recognition. It is not to impress but rather to express who I am.

I remember as a young woman asking a dear, older friend how to live from a place of genuineness and honesty. I was looking for advice that would relate to me, not only as a singer, but as a person. Her response sticks with me to this day: "It is as we have been taught, honesty is the best policy. Be true to who you are. Speak to any situation as clearly as possible. Avoid over-gesturing and facial affectations, which detract from what you want to share. Let yes or no be enough without a lot of explanation. If there is space for giving reason to any question, be prepared by knowing yourself and what is essentially important to you. Live in integrity." These ideas resonated with me and I knew I needed to be able to be face-to-face with myself and others. In this is the intimacy of honesty.

Although much of my singing career has been in sacred music, I've always admired the insight of songwriters from every genre. I especially like Billy Joel; something about him always reminded me of my older brother, God Rest his Soul, who was a lover of jazz piano.

"Honesty"[1]

If you search for tenderness
It isn't hard to find
You can have the love you need to live
if you look for truthfulness
You might just as well be blind
It always seems to be so hard to give

Honesty is such a lonely word
Everyone is so untrue
Honesty is hardly ever heard
And mostly what I need from you

I can always find someone
To say they sympathize
If I wear my heart out on my sleeve
But I don't want some pretty face
To tell me pretty lies
All I want is someone to believe

Perhaps the most significant life lesson singing has taught me is how to see through the innate charade and see myself as I really am in order to live in truth, create my own story, sing my own song, and share my own journey. One of the best exercises ever suggested to me by a vocal coach was to stand in front of a mirror and sing my song directly into my eyes without flinching or looking away. The intimate honesty of this practice continually amazes me. Am I believable? As I focus on a genuine and natural presentation, any message is conveyed with authenticity because I'm in the zone of my being. Face-to-face contact has been for me, one of the best ways to determine whether or not I feel the gentle, soft beauty of being honest and real.

There were lofty and noble dreams and a hope for life's best that pushed me down the road to achievement. However, when dreams were suspect and hopes were threatened, confusion got in the way

---

1 "Honesty" (1979), which was solely written by Billy Joel, talks about the inherent lack of honesty even in the closest of relationships. The implication is that you know someone really cares for you when they "call you out on your stuff. Retrieved from en.wikipedia.org/wiki/Honesty_(Billy_Joel_song)

of honest creative flow. It took time to figure out the cause for such struggle and confusion. When I allowed the most valuable lesson of all to awaken in my soul, the unique truth of who I am, the inner curiosity about myself and vocal technique began to be satisfied. I was introduced to the real person infused with a mystical sense of being, the musical vibration of self full of energy. The harder I tried to be what I wanted to be, the more difficult it became. My trying was eventually replaced with a willingness to surrender to all effort, submit to the process all along the journey, accept input and criticism as a good thing, grow through it all and never give up on the desire in my soul. Being open to learn assisted me in finding myself in spite of limitations, and allowed me to honor the unique, authentic person living and singing with honesty and truth. The personal rewards and healing have been beyond belief. The love of singing without the need for recognition and all the life gifts along the way are what I give freely to the listener. It is in the giving that my joy is full.

ABOUT THE AUTHOR: Ruthe Hanson Plaché is an author, speaker, musician and coach with a wide range of creative and humanistic interests. She is an artist who loves gardening, a Certified Life Coach, an Ordained Minister, NLP Practitioner and Theta Healing Facilitator. She is also Certified in RCFE Administration/Senior Living, licensed in Cosmetology, and has a BA in Music. Ruth describes her life's work as that of an "encourager," supporting one's individuality and unique self-expression with respect and unconditional love. Her love of diversity has led her to travel the world and host over one hundred international students, though her first priority has always been her four children and four grandchildren.

Ruthe Hanson Plaché
"With a Song in My Heart"
Ruthe.me
ruthe36@yahoo.com

My Flow is Purposeful and Divine

Sharon Plaché

When I feel the warmth of the sun on my back, I am grateful it is being itself. Listening to the birds sing their song, I appreciate they are who they are. As I see the beauty of nature in all its infinite forms, I respect each expression as purposeful.

If only women were valued as much for their authentic selves. All too often, we are pressured to be something or do something other than who and what we truly are. This pressure seems to come from everywhere—the media, religion, politics, and social norms, all telling us who we are supposed to be, what we are supposed to do, and what we can and cannot have in our lives.

What if we lived in a world where we could only survive if we lived as the authentic self? Where, if we were something other than that, we would be unable to function, like a computer that crashes when it is infected with a virus, unable to function as it was created and designed to.

Sounds like science fiction, right? But the truth is, like that computer, when we behave based on external norms and demands, we are undermining our survival and most definitely our ability to thrive. I began to ask myself, why have I so often tried to be something else, someone else? When did I start trying to fit into someone else's mold? What am I missing out on when I am being what others want? And, when I am not being myself, who am I? When I am being myself, who am I not?

The challenge to be who we really are begins even before birth.

Over the years, I've heard several pregnant friends and family members saying whether they wanted a boy or a girl; some even expressed disappointment to find out it was the other. Sounds innocent enough, right? We want what we want. However, in studying the power of influence and imprinting on the human psyche, I have learned that even in the womb we can feel made "wrong" and that we should be something other than what we are.

Of course, we all choose what environment to come into: parents, cultures, family dynamics, and so on, each offering contrast and support as we grow. To me, the real question is, "How can I determine the 'I am' of myself, independent of the overbearing influences of others?"

I appreciate the need for structure in an orderly, safe society; yet it seems to go much further than that. We are being molded according to an arbitrary set of demands. I began asking myself, "What would happen if I trusted myself to tune into the innate 'homing' device of the unique spirit/soul and express who and what I really am?" Maybe answering this question is the gift to ourselves and our world that we all are seeking.

When I started studying Neuro Linguistic Programming (NLP), which I now teach, I found a wonderful presupposition that "everyone has their own model of the world." This is the first step to respecting others' points of view and how it helps to build community. Even more profound was to identify the values in my life that really drive my course and commitment in life. This was amazing to me to dig down and identify my values from inside, rather than from an external application of the "shoulds," "musts," and "have-tos" that were a staple during my developmental years.

I grew up in a very strict religious environment, with my parents, three brothers, and a Patriarchal Godhead. Needless to say the rules of life were very specific and expectations of me very defined. There was little room for self-discovery or expression. To question others or even myself was not allowed, yet I still felt deep inside that many of these external dictates were discordant with who I really was. It was not until my early twenties, however, that I felt I could push the boundaries of this world.

My feelings were best illustrated by Sue Monk Kidd's book, *"The Dance of the Dissident Daughter: A Woman's Journey from Christian Tradition to the Sacred Feminine."* Here are a couple of quotes that really spoke to me then, and now.

"Women themselves condition their daughters to serve the system of male primacy. If a daughter challenges it, the mother will generally defend the system rather than her daughter. These mothers, victims themselves, have unwittingly become wounded wounders. Women need to attack culture's oppression of women, for there truly is a godlike socializing power that induces women to "buy in" or collude, but we also need to confront our own part in accepting male dominance and take responsibility where appropriate."

"There's something infinitely sad about little girls who grow up understanding (usually unconsciously) that if God is male, it's because male is the most valuable thing to be. This belief resonates in a thousand hidden ways in their lives. It slowly cripples girl children, and it cripples female adults."

This patriarchal dogma was pervasive in my youth. However, instead of crippling me, it led me to seek a greater understanding of the feminine and her many experiences of tenderness and power. It led me to become a feminist, a label I proudly wear today. I am an advocate for women and girls—their safety, health, education, and infinite opportunities. This does not mean I am against men; it means I am for balance and equality, something this world is sorely lacking.

I recently finishing hosting a Power of 8 Group, based on the book by Lynne McTaggart, with thirteen amazing women. I was so inspired by the courage, strength, and love of my soul sisters, as well as their fragility, vulnerability, and tenderness, as we all sought support and love to actualize our greatest potential.

A significant question in the group was, "Where and when can I be real about all the amazing and all the messy?" Authenticity is a moment of being myself as I am in that moment, being witnessed and able to witness others in return; letting it be okay to "not" be okay; and safe to show life's raw and challenging moments as well as the magic and successes.

This begged the question, how can true self-acceptance and love exist if I have to always be okay, put together, living a successful, creative strategy in my life. What happens when I am all that and still not okay, or unable or ready to "fix" or resolve it? What if this painful storm I'm in the middle of is also bearing gifts I'm not yet aware of?

The year 2018 was a particularly challenging one for me. I navigated through high surfs, choppy waters, barren deserts, and steep mountains. I was lonely, uncertain, and overwhelmed beyond measure. I had to witness the immense suffering of my parents, my partner, and myself. It was near impossible to do any fixing; I couldn't even explain it to someone else.

The raw intensity of these experiences cut me to the bone and demanded brutal honesty. I was forced to tell the truth to myself and others about who I am, what I need, and what I will and will not participate in. This was not the first time in my life I'd had to examine and address these issues; however, this year required that I take a deeper dive into the "who I am" than ever before. Again I asked myself, "What do I want to BE?"; "How do I want to DO it?"; "What do I want to HAVE in my life?," then I let the answers flow from my core values and essence of the greater Self.

Life has offered me many homecoming moments, but this time the clarity was even deeper in terms of honoring what I authentically need and desire; what I will not tolerate; what I am creating; and who will share in those creations.

I found great inspiration in the work of Dr. Brené Brown, who wrote about the *"...raw courage to be me whether others accept, agree or even like me. The most dangerous stories we make up are the narratives that diminish our inherent worthiness. We must reclaim the truth about our lovability, divinity, and creativity."*

Dr. Brown's message has been a great reminder that forgoing myself for someone else's purpose is always abusive, destructive, and futile. It has taken some time, but I have come to be more comfortable with this understanding and how it impacts myself and others. I must feel good first, regardless of the outcome.

Over thirty years ago, while still in my twenties, I set my career course in the healing arts; I wanted to feel better about myself and help others feel better as well. However, in order to be a care provider for others, one must first and always be "okay."

In the process of being a peacemaker and care provider for the family and clients, I have learned to take great care of myself, create boundaries and honor myself. Yet, there were still areas of my life and myself that hurt and posed challenges. I felt I had to be super human/super woman. This too has been excavated, revealing a deeper clarity, strength, purpose, and guiding light for my choices. I delved into parts of me I didn't know existed and investigated what I truly need, no questions asked.

Most girls and women are taught to be agreeable, accommodating, solicitous, gracious, and kind. When we say "no," "not interested," or "not now," we are blamed and shamed as emotional or unreasonable, or referred to as prudes, ice queens, or bitches. Nowhere is this better illustrated than in Eve Ensler's brave creation, *The Vagina Monologues*. I have seen the stage production several times, and I am always impressed by its powerful message about both the suppression and the power of women.

"Whether she's in Africa or the suburban malls of America there is an underlying theme in the lives of girls: pleasing. There's an overall mandate that girls are meant to please. There are so many ways girls are still being pressured to be something else, somebody else's idea of what they should be. How do girls break away from pleasing others?"

"I want to change the verb 'to please' to some other verb—engage

or create or educate or imagine. I want girls to take responsibility for who they are."

We all have an innate desire to create and experience pleasure; however, it is often for others, and at our own expense. For me, the shift came after a major back surgery ten years ago. I started living by my own "Pleasure Principle," deciding that something must first feel good and be pleasing to me, otherwise it was not worth creating or participating in.

I also realized that when it is good for me, it is always good for others. This has helped me honor myself more and allow my own authentic voice and preferences to emerge. I recognize that my own needs and desires are Divine and thus have purpose for myself and all creation.

I have always found the following questions from the NLP tradition to unearth powerful a-ha moments; indeed, I still ask them of myself.

-What happens when I am what others want or expect?

-What would happen if I am not being what others want or expect?

-What doesn't happen when I am what others want or expect?

-What doesn't happen when I am not being what others want or expect?

The journey continues, and it is truly a never-ending love story into deeper levels of Homecoming and Celebration of my Authentic Self and all Her Gifts, Talents, Virtues, and Magic. It allows me to have a clearer understanding of Who I desire to BE, How I desire to DO it, and What I desire to HAVE.

As it is possible for me, may it be possible for all of my Soul Sisters and All Creation.

Namaste.

ABOUT THE AUTHOR: Sharon Plaché is a bestselling author and intuitive teacher, coach, and healer passionate about empowering clients to discover, grow, and create in all areas of their lives. Since 1989 she has maintained a private practice, offering a myriad of healing modalities including MER® Mental & Emotional Release, ThetaHealing®, Innerwise®, and Hypnosis; she is also an NLP instructor, practitioner, and mentor. Her retreat center in San Diego offers trainings, aquatic bodywork, therapeutic massage, yoga, meditation, and more. Sharon is grateful to be a practitioner for the Wave Academy, which offers support to Veterans with PTSD.

Sharon Plaché
SharonPlache.com
info@sharonplache.com
619-339-8177

About the Authors

**Are you inspired by the stories in this book?
Let the authors know.**

**See the contact information at the end of each chapter
and reach out to them.**

They'd love to hear from you!

Author Rights & Disclaimer

*Each author in this book retains the copyright and all inherent
rights to their individual chapter. Their stories are printed herein
with each author's permission.*

*Each author is responsible for the individual opinions expressed
through their words. Powerful You! Publishing bears no
responsibility for the content of the stories by these authors.*

Acknowledgements & Gratitude

We are grateful for the bounty of beautiful individuals who grace the days of our lives and who honor us with their presence, connection, love, support, and guidance.

To our authors, who enthusiastically and fearlessly share your raw, unique, and authentic selves, we thank you and applaud you. You're making this world a more loving place simply by following your own purpose and calling. You've provided us with renewed courage and confidence in our own mission, and we know you as champions of spirit.

To our team and behind-the-scenes consultants who give openly of themselves and their expertise and provide guidance and loving support as well as the wisdom of years of experience, we thank you.

To our editor, Dana Micheli, we thank you for your unique insights and loving commitment in assisting our authors to shine. You Rock!

To our trainers Kathy Sipple, AmondaRose Igoe, Linda Albright, we thank you for your dedication and expertise. We love each of you.

To Lisa Winston, our dear friend and enlightened soul sister who wrote the Foreword, we thank you for the simplicity and honesty with which you approach each moment of life and business, love and connection. Your words light the way for all of us to experience life authentically.

To our friends and families, your support and love are more precious than you know. You help us to live more fully into the lives we desire and encourage us to reach for the stars. We love you deeply.

Above all, we are humbled by the never-ending flow of spiritual support we receive from angels on earth and beyond. This book is yet another reminder of spirit in action and the amazing strength and fortitude afforded to us in each moment.

Namaste` and Blessings, Love, and Gratitude,
Sue Urda and Kathy Fyler

About Sue Urda and Kathy Fyler

Sue and Kathy have been friends for 29 years and business partners since 1994. They have received many awards and accolades for their businesses over the years and continue to love the work they do and the people they do it with. As publishers, they are honored to help people share their stories, passions, and lessons.

Their mission is to raise the vibration of people and the planet and to connect and empower women in their lives. Their calling has been years in the making and is a gift from Spirit.

The strength of their partnership lies in their deep respect, love, and understanding of one another as well as their complementary skills and knowledge. Kathy is a technology enthusiast, web goddess, and free-thinker. Sue is an author and speaker with a love of creative undertakings. Their honor, love, and admiration for each other are boundless.

Together their energies combine to feed the flames of countless women who are seeking truth, empowerment, joy, peace, and connection with themselves, their own spirits, and other women.

Connect with Sue and Kathy:

Powerful You! Inc.
239-280-0111
info@powerfulyou.com
PowerfulYouPublishing.com
SueUrda.com

About Lisa Winston

Lisa Winston is a gifted vocalist, #1 international bestselling author of "Your Turning Point," TV host and inspirational speaker. A life of extreme challenges, including losing her home to wildfire and breast cancer, made her hungry for a deeper connection to Source and determined to find her true calling. Today, she shares the message that life is always happening *for* you and challenges are sent to refine, not define you.

Lisa has produced many influential global summits and live events and is featured on online summits, national radio, podcasts and trainings. She was recently featured on her first magazine cover for *The Global Voice.* She co-hosts and produces *The Mindset Reset TV Show,* a weekly series which reaches millions, worldwide.

Lisa is so blessed to be mom to her beautiful daughter, Sarah, and to live, travel, and work with her soulmate and life partner, Dr. Joe Vitale.

CONNNECT WITH LISA:
LisaWinston.com
MindsetResetTV.com
thebeautyofauthenticity@gmail.com
Facebook (personal): facebook.com/lisa.winston.501
Facebook (biz): facebook.com/lisawinstoncoach
Twitter: twitter.com/LisaAWinston
Linked In: linkedin.com/in/lisa-winston-853bb826
Instagram: instagram.com/lisawinston

Are You Called to be an Author?

If you're like most people, you may find the prospect of writing a book daunting. Where to begin? How to proceed? No worries! We're here to help.

Whether you choose to write your own book, contribute to an anthology, or be part of our Wisdom & Insights book series using our QuickPublish Formula™, we'll be your guiding light, professional consultant, and enthusiastic supporter. If you can see yourself as an author partnering with a publishing company who has your best interest at heart and with the expertise to back it up, we're the publisher for you.

We provide personalized guidance through the writing and editing process. We offer complete publishing packages and our service is designed for a personal and optimal authoring experience.

We are committed to helping individuals express their voices and shine their lights into the world. Are you ready to start your journey as an author? Do it with Powerful You! Publishing.

Powerful You! Publishing
239-280-0111
powerfulyoupublishing.com

Anthology Books

Empowering Transformations for Women
Women Living Consciously
Journey to Joy
Pathways to Vibrant Health & Well-Being
Women Living Consciously Book II
Healthy, Abundant, and Wise
Keys to Conscious Business Growth
The Gifts of Grace & Gratitude
Heal Thy Self
Empower Your Life
Heart & Soul

Other Books

Powerful Intentions, Everyday Gratitude - Books I & II
Let Me Walk the Journey with You
Medicine Jewelry – Working with Rock People
Led By Purpose
Divinely Fit
A Journey Back to Restoration
Seven Sundays to Sweet Inner Serenity
Live Beyond Your Loss
Frankie: My Brother, My Hero
The Power of Love and Awakening Consciousness

Live Open.
Live Free.

May You Always
Honor the Whispers
Of Your Soul.